P9-EDU-448

Colombo's
101 CANADIAN PLACES

Colombo's
101 CANADIAN PLACES

John Robert Colombo

Drawings by Peter Whalley

Hounslow Press

Colombo's 101 Canadian Places

ISBN 0-88882-069-0

Publisher: Anthony Hawke
Designer: Gerard Williams
Printer: Weller Publishing Company Limited

Publication was assisted by
The Canada Council
and The Ontario Arts Council.

Hounslow Press
A Division of Anthony R. Hawke Limited
124 Parkview Avenue
Willowdale, Ontario, Canada
M2N 3Y5

Printed in Canada.

Place names had always been the most permanent things in the short little human story.
Hugh MacLennan, *Voices in Time* (1980)

The astronomers have discovered a peculiar spot on Saturn and are greatly excited over it. Yet there are plenty of peculiar spots no farther away than Okotoks and Claresholm.
Bob Edwards, *The Eye Opener,* July 18, 1903

If we go far enough down this road we'll find Nineveh.
A.Y. Jackson, to interviewer, July 17, 1961

PREFACE

This book is a cavalcade of Canadian places, a canter across the length and breadth of the country in quest of capital cities, commercial centres, uncommonly named communities, and historic sites.

Here are 101 Canadian places, all of interest. They range from Alert (N.W.T.) to Yoho (B.C.); from the small, Punkeydoodles Corners (Ont.), to the large, Montreal (Que.); from the odd, Dildo (Nfld.), to the unusual, Saint-Louis-du-Ha! Ha! (Que.). Each place has its entry and for each place there is a little etymology, history, lore, and learning. The tone is light-hearted, though the temper somewhat ironic. The chances are, no matter where you were born or where you now reside or where you aspire to live, a community here is of concern to you.

So vast a land is Canada that when examining its communities, whether metropolitan or rural, one might overlook the fact that, in size, this country ranks as the world's second-largest (with the Soviet Union preceding it and China following it). In terms of population (there were estimated to be 24,739,400 Canadians on January 1, 1983), the country does not place among the top twenty of the 200-odd countries that make up the world. Canadians may be dense when it comes to certain things, but population density is not one of them. There is so much land and there are so few people that the density is roughly four people for every square mile (or ten for every square kilometre). There is a kid's riddle which runs —

Question: Why are Torontonians so stupid?
Answer: Because the population is densest there!

In point of fact, the densest Canadians, in terms of crowding, are those on Prince Edward Island. Although hard to believe during a Vancouver or Toronto rush hour, Canada is an uncrowded country.

Extremes of all sorts appeals to the popular mind. Here are Canada's geographical extremities. The southernmost point is Middle Island in Lake Erie. In a straight line 2,875 miles (4,627 km) northward, past the treeline and far into the Arctic, is Cape Columbia on Ellesmere Island, Canada's northernmost point. From east to west at the widest point, the straight-line distance is 3,223 miles (5,187 km) from Cape Spear, Nfld., to Mount St. Elias, Y.T.

When figures fail to bring home the scale of a country, relative sizes often succeed. Given here are the areas of the country and of its component parts in comparison with the areas of selected other countries. All figures refer to square miles. (For those who think in metric rather than imperial measure, the rule of thumb for conversion from square miles to square kilometres is to multiply the former by 2.5899 to reach the latter.) Here goes ......

Canada itself, comprising 3,850,790, is smaller than the Soviet Union (8,647,249) but larger than China (3,690,546).

Alberta, with 248,800, is larger than Somalia (246,000) but smaller than Afghanistan (250,000).

British Columbia, with 359,279, is larger than Venezuela (352,150) but smaller than Tanzania (362,820).

Manitoba, with 211,775, is about the size of France (211,152).

New Brunswick, with 27,835, is larger than Ireland (26,559) but smaller than Scotland (30,412).

Newfoundland, with 143,045, is larger than Congo (132,000) but smaller than Zimbabwe (150,333).

Nova Scotia, with 20,402, is larger than Costa Rica (19,650) but smaller than Togo (22,000).

Ontario, with 344,092, is larger than Turkey (296,503) but smaller than Nigeria (356,574).

Prince Edward Island, with 2,184, is larger than Trinidad and Tobago (1,980) but smaller than Cyprus (3,572).

Quebec, with 523,860, is larger than South Africa (471,320) but smaller than Tibet (560,000).

Saskatchewan, with 220,182, is larger than Spain (194,834) but smaller than Kenya (225,000).

The Northwest Territories and the Yukon Territory, combined, with 1,458,784, are somewhat larger than India (1,261,483).

A mammoth among nations, a mote among peoples. "We live in an empty place filled with wonders," said Peter C. Newman. "And someday," added George Whalley, "somebody will find a market for muskeg."

ACKNOWLEDGEMENTS

Numerous acknowledgements are in order. For information on places and names, I am indebted to *The National Atlas of Canada* (4th rev. ed., 1974), edited by Gerald Fremlin; for general information, *Canada Year Book 1976-77* (special edition, 1977). The main source of the etymologies is William B. Hamilton's indispensible *The Macmillan Book of Canadian Place Names* (1978) and of the locales *The Encyclopedia Canadiana* (1958, 1963). Especially useful is the series of illustrated volumes issued by the Reader's Digest Association in cooperation with the Canadian Automobile Association: *Explore Canada* (1974), *Scenic Wonders of Canada* (1976), *Heritage of Canada* (1978), *Canadian Book of the Road* (1979), and *Drive North America* (1983). I also turned to *Colombo's Canadian Quotations* (1974), *Colombo's Canadian References* (1976), and *Colombo's Book of Canada* (1978). Not all the information came from popular sources but from years of research in libraries and archives. The population figures are from the 1981 Census, except for figures qualified by the year 1983 (in which case they are Statistics Canada's estimates for January 1 of that year).

I wish to express my thanks to the following friends and colleagues: Philip Singer, Michael Richardson, and N. Dipu Choudhuri of the Bathurst Heights Area Branch, North York Public Library; Joel Bonn, Evelyn Wood Reading Dynamics, Montreal; Kamala Bhatia, Humanities Division, Mohawk College, Hamilton; Diane Mew, Toronto; Peter Whalley, Morin Heights, Que.; and Anthony R. Hawke, publisher, Hounslow Press, Toronto. Ever-helpful was Alan Rayburn, Executive Secretary of the Canadian Permanent Committee on Geographical Names, Ottawa; although he is a colleague from way back, neither Rayburn nor the committee of which he is a member is to be held responsible for statements of fact or opinion expressed by the author.

ATLAS
Canada
THS
ALERT
YOHO
NORTH
PUNKEYDOODLES

ALERT, N.W.T.

Alert is a weather and signals station located at the northern tip of Ellesmere Island overlooking the Arctic Ocean. It is the world's most northern settlement, located some 500 miles (800 km) from the North Pole and closer to Moscow than to Montreal. The Canadian government, which established Alert in 1950 for undefined communications and military purposes, named it after the H.M.S. *Alert,* flagship of the British survey expedition to the Arctic in 1875-76.

There is a sign at Alert which reads: "There is no place anything like this place, anywhere near this place, so this must be the place: Alert."

It is hard not to conclude that Canadians should be more alert.

AMHERST, N.S.

Amherst, near the New Brunswick border, was named in 1759 for Lord Jeffrey Amherst, then commander of the British forces, later Governor General of British North America. It became a town in 1889 and has a population of 9,684.

Perhaps Amherst's most celebrated visitor was Oscar Wilde, who lectured on aesthetics at the Academy of Music in 1882. "I would rather have discovered Mrs. Langtry than have discovered America," he told a reporter. "When I was young I thought the Wars of the Roses were to decide whether a red or a white rose was the most beautiful. I learned afterwards that it was a vulgar dispute." He went on to name Canada's leading poets: Louis Fréchette, Charles G.D. Roberts, and Pelham Mulvany ("a man once well known at Trinity College").

Its most notorious temporary resident was Leon Trotsky. The Russian revolutionary and his family were forcibly removed from a Norwegian vessel at Halifax; Trotsky's wife and children were kept under close surveillance in Halifax while Trotsky was incarcerated in a prisoner-of-war camp at Amherst, April 3-29, 1917. Upon his release, he sailed back to Russia where he played a prominent role in the October Revolution. "We were put through an examination the like of which I had never before experienced, even in the

Peter-Paul fortress (of St. Petersburg). For in the Czar's fortress the police stripped me and searched me in privacy, whereas here our democratic allies subjected us to this shameful humiliation before a dozen men." Trotsky was no doubt familiar with Dostoyevsky's observation: "The degree of civilization in a society can be judged by entering its prisons."

ANTIGONISH, N.S.

Located on the north shore of Nova Scotia, midway between Halifax and Sydney, it attracted Gaelic-speaking Scots early in its history. Its name may derive from the Micmac *Nalegitkoonechk* ("where branches are torn off") which, with varied spellings, was recorded as early as 1672. The present population is 5,205.

The pride of the town — and of Canada — is the world-famous Antigonish Movement, a co-operative, self-help movement that grew out of an extension program at St. Francis Xavier University. Since its founding in 1921, it has spread to many Third World countries. Father James J. Tompkins of St. FX supplied the basic philosophy: "The people make giants."

BADDECK, N.S.

Baddeck is the name of a village, a bay, and a river. The name is a corruption of the Micmac *Petekook* for "place that lies on the backward turn on the river." Baddeck is the centre of the beautiful Bras d'Or region of Cape Breton Island.

Alexander Graham Bell lived and worked here each summer from 1885 to his death in 1922. He called his estate Beinn Bhreagh, which is Gaelic for "beautiful mountain." The estate is private property but the museum in Alexander Graham Bell National Historic Park is full of devices for air and sea transporation designed by the inventor of the telephone. Here is his *Silver Dart* which achieved an elevation of thirty feet in 1909. Here is *Hydrodrome-4*, the world's earliest hydrofoil, which attained a speed of over 70 miles per hour later that year.

BAFFIN ISLAND, N.W.T.

The largest of the Arctic Islands and the most eastern, it was discovered by the explorer William Baffin in 1616 and named after him (although not officially until 1905). In 1975, Auyuittuq National Park was opened on the Island; the name means, in Inuktitut, "land of the big ice." The Island has a permanent population of 3,378.

On 1 July 1909, Captain Joseph-Elzéar Bernier claimed the Arctic archipelago for Canada. Here is how he did it. "I took possession of Baffin Island for Canada in the presence of several Eskimo, and after firing nineteen shots I instructed an Eskimo to fire the twentieth, telling him that he was now a Canadian."

BANFF, Alta

The sight of Banff nestling in the Bow River Valley amid the towering Rocky Mountains must be one of the finest views the world has to offer. The focal point of the scene is the historic Banff Springs Hotel, built in the chateau style in 1912, where many distinguished visitors have enjoyed their holiday in Banff National Park, the country's oldest.

Banff was named for the ancient resort town in Scotland, close to the birthplace of Sir George Stephen, president of the CPR. The resort of Jasper, in Jasper National Park, was named after a NWC clerk Jasper Hawes; and Lake Louise honours Princess Louise Caroline Alberta, wife of the Governor General the Marquess of Lorne.

Banff never looked better on film than it does in *The Forty-Ninth Parallel,* directed by Michael Powell and released in 1941, which follows the flight across the country of marooned German seamen. It stars Laurence Olivier as a French-Canadian trapper and Leslie Howard as an effete Englishman. The scenes in Banff are particularly well handled.

In the 1930s, Greta Garbo addressed a postcard view of Banff to her friend Lars Saxon and wrote on the back: "This is just one of the many wonderful places you'll see on your way to C."

BIGGAR, Sask.

Biggar, located on the railway line west of Saskatoon, is a prairie town with a population of 2,561. It was named after William Hodgins Biggar, chief solicitor of the Grand Trunk. It was incorporated as a village in 1909 and as a town in 1911.

What is fondly remembered about Biggar is the sign the townsfolk erected in the 1940s with the grand pun: NEW YORK IS BIG, BUT THIS IS BIGGAR.

BLOMIDON, N.S.

The village of Blomidon on the shore of Minas Basin is said to owe its name to a corruption of the nautical phrase "blow me down" (which refers to a downrush of wind from an escarpment which could capsize a small vessel). Extending into Minas Basin north of the village is Cape Blomidon, which is 670 feet (201 m) in height and the traditional home of Glooscap. The Micmac culture hero brought happiness to the Indians, then sailed away in his great stone canoe, singing a strange sad song, but promising to return.

BON ECHO, ONT.

Bon Echo Provincial Park, near Kaladar in eastern Ontario, was opened in 1961. The park is adjacent to Upper Mazinaw Lake and Lower Mazinaw Lake out of which juts Mazinaw Rock — a Precambrian outcropping a mile long (1.4 km) and 400 feet (120 m) high. The historic rock, which Algonkian Indians decorated with pictographs, is now known as "Old Walt." On August 25, 1919, the southern end of the rock was dedicated to the "democratic ideals" of Walt Whitman by a circle of admirers of the American poet. Inscribed on the face of the rock are the following lines from Whitman's "Song of Myself": "My foothold is tenon'd and mortised in granite/I laugh at what you call dissolution/And I know the amplitude of time." The Algonkian name for the area, *Ma-si-nog*, or "place of writing," became Mazinaw. The name Bon Echo dates from 1899 and refers to the acoustical properties of the area where as many as seven echoes have been heard.

BRANDON, Man.

Situated on the Assiniboine River, Brandon is the oldest prairie city west of Winnipeg. It was originally an HBC post, built in 1793 and named Brandon House, after the Duke of Brandon, a shareholder. Named in 1881, it achieved city status in 1882, and now has a population of 36,242.

"Some of Canada's provinces were acquired by adoption. On others the status was conferred after a rigorously supervised apprenticeship. Manitoba was simply conjured into being." So wrote the historian F.A. Milligan in 1950.

The science-fiction writer E. Mayne Hull, one-time secretary to farmleader Henry Wise Wood and author of *Planets for Sale* (1954) and *The Winged Man* (1966), in collaboration with her husband A.E. van Vogt, was born in Brandon in 1905. She died in Los Angeles, California, in 1975.

BURGEO, Nfld.

The name Burgeo is held to be a corruption of Virgeo, or "virgin." A 1536 map identifies a group of islands off the southwestern coast of Newfoundland as Mill Virgines. Why so many virgins? William B. Hamilton explains the etymology: "The name was bestowed in commemoration of the eleven thousand virgins who, on returning from Rome, are believed to have been killed by the Huns at Cologne in the 4th or 5th century." The name drifted to the outport as Virgeo and evolved into Burgeo. Today the fishing community is a town of 2,504.

Burgeo's most famous "come-from-away" residents were the writer Farley Mowat and his wife Claire who, between 1962 and 1967, watched the twentieth century invade this isolated fishing community with telephone, television and the Trans-Island Highway. Mowat's views are set forth in *A Whale for the Killing* (1972) and his wife's fictional memoir is called *The Outport People* (1983).

CALGARY, Alta.

Calgary is located in the Bow Valley at the confluence of the Bow and Elbow rivers, where the plains end and the foothills of the

Rockies begin. It dates back to Fort Brisebois, founded by the NWMP in 1875, and was named Calgary the following year. The name refers to a location on the Isle of Mull, Scotland, and may be Gaelic for "clear running water" or "stone enclosure." Calgary became a town in 1884 and a city in 1893. The population is 592,743.

It has been estimated that close to half the total population of the city is employed by the petroleum industry. With the rise in oil prices in the 1970s, the city came into its own. For the first time Toronto was eclipsed by another city as the butt of bad jokes — "the city we love to hate" — Calgary.

It is generally agreed that for stylishly dressed businesswomen, Calgary ranks second in the country (after Montreal with its French sophistication and chic). For Stetson hats it ranks first.

The city is famous for the Calgary Stampede which, since 1912, has been held annually for ten days in July. Rodeo events, livestock shows, and general amusements vie with the ever-popular chuck-wagon race (first run at the Stampede).

CAMPOBELLO ISLAND, N.B.

The name of this island, which lies near the entrance of Passamoquoddy Bay in the Bay of Fundy one mile from the coast of Maine, is a pleasant pun on that of Governor Lord William Campbell of Nova Scotia. The name goes back to 1770 and describes the ambience of the island, which has a resident population of 1,424.

Campobello Island will forever be identified with FDR. Here is where Franklin Delano Roosevelt spent the summers between 1883 and 1921. The family's Dutch-colonial, 32-room "summer cottage" is the centrepiece of Roosevelt Campobello International Park. FDR called Campobello Island his "Beloved Island."

CANADA

One of the world's largest countries, Canada occupies much of the northern half of the North American continent. It has an area of 3,851,809 square miles (9,976,139 km^2) and is more than 40 times the size of Britain and 18 times the size of France. The population on January 1, 1983, was estimated to be 24,739,400. There is no permanent settlement in approximately 89% of the country. Over three-quaters of the population live in an urban rather than a rural environment.

The word "Canada" may have derived from the Iroquoian word *kanata,* which means "village" or "community." It first appeared in print in Jacques Cartier's account of his voyage of 1535, where it was used to designate a region along the St. Lawrence River between present-day Quebec City and the mouth of the river. Over the centuries its use broadened, until, on July 1, 1867, it came to be applied to the Dominion of Canada.

The historian A.R.M. Lower said, "Canada is a supreme act of faith." "Canada is the only country in the world that knows how to live without an identity," suggested Marshall McLuhan. Interviewed in Buenos Aires, the Argentine writer Jorge Luis Borges noted, "Canada is so far away it hardly exists."

There is no place currently called Canada in the Dominion of Canada though there is a Canada Bay on the eastern shore of

northern Newfoundland, not ot mention three Canada Creeks — in New Brunswick's Albert County, in Nova Scotia northwest of Kentville, and near the Tyre Valley of Prince Edward Island.

Elsewhere in the world appear these other Canadas:

Canadaway is the original name of the village of Fredonia in upstate New York. Also in upstate New York are Canada Lake, Canadarego Lake, and West Canadian River.

Canadensis is a town in northeast Pennsylvania.

Canadian is a town in northwest Texas, located on the Canadian River.

Cañada de Gomez, Cañada Honda, and Cañada Verde are three towns in central Argentina. (A *cañada,* in Spanish, is a "canyon.")

Kanada, sometimes Kannada, is a district in southwest India; a Dravidian language spoken by 18 million people; and a second-century Hindu philosopher.

Kanaka is a Polynesian word meaning "man," used by Polynesians to describe themselves.

CARCROSS, Y.T.

Carcross, located on the north end of Bennett Lake, is "the town that discovered the Klondike." It was the point of departure for George Carmack, Skookum Jim, and Tagish Charlie, whose gold strike at Bonanza Creek, a tributary of the Klondike River, on August 17, 1896, sparked the Klondike Gold Rush.

It was originally called Caribou Crossing, a reference to the movement of caribou. The contraction was coined by Bishop William Bompas and approved by the names authority in 1905. The community has a post office, a mission, and an RCMP detachment, with a 1976 population of 175.

CASTLE MOUNTAIN, Alta.

Changing the name of Castle Mountain in Banff National Park to Mount Eisenhower was one of Prime Minister Mackenzie King's least-inspired and least-popular decisions. He made the change in

1946 to honour Dwight D. Eisenhower, Supreme Allied Commander in the Second World War, and in doing so he set many teeth on edge.

Not only was the original name for the mountain historic — it went back to 1858 — but it was descriptive of this 9,076 foot (2,722 m) peak, which resembles a fortress with parapets. The Alpine Club of Canada suggested some better way could be found to honour Eisenhower than by renaming "the landmark which is fittingly named."

The original name of Castle Mountain was restored in December 1979, during the last month of the Clark administration. After a number of appeals and petitions, the governments of Alberta and Canada took this action, reserving Eisenhower's name for the mountain's most prominent (but not its highest) point — Eisenhower Peak.

CAVENDISH, P.E.I.

The village of Cavendish, on the north shore of Prince Edward Island, was named by a local resident to honour his patron Lord Frederick Cavendish. A post office, originally established here in 1833, has since 1953 been called Green Gables.

Cavendish inspired the fictional community of Avonlea which is the setting of the eight "Anne" books by L.M. Montgomery. The first of these was *Anne of Green Gables* (1908), and the original Green Gables at Cavendish is a charming, green-and-white house in which the author visited as a child and where she wrote her children's classic. Her gravesite is nearby. Green Gables is part of Prince Edward Island National Park and the most popular literary shrine in Canada.

L.M. Montgomery addressed the Toronto Women's Press Club before her death in 1942 and said: "The critics condemn my books because of what they call my lack of realism. My reply to them is that sunsets are just as real as pigsties and I prefer writing about sunsets."

Ice Station CESAR, N.W.T.

The acronym CESAR stands for the Canadian Expedition to Study the Alpha Ridge. When it was operational, in April and May 1983, CESAR consisted of a dozen or so scientists living in twenty-four red, white, and blue nylon tents erected on the frozen Arctic Ocean. The location was 295 miles (475 km) from the North Pole and 370 miles (600 km) from the nearest land — the northern tip of Ellesmere Island. The scientists were engaged in a study of the Alpha Ridge, a mountain range as large as the Alps, submerged beneath the Arctic Ocean, that extends from Ellesmere Island to Siberia. Before the spring thaw, the average temperature at Ice Station CESAR was the point at which the imperial and metric systems converge: minus 40 degress. For two months this tent city was the most northerly scientific community in the world.

CHARLOTTETOWN, P.E.I.

Charlottetown is located on the south shore of the Island. The French settled at Port La Jolie, across the harbour at present Rocky Point, in 1720. The British arrived and named their settlement Charlotte Town in 1765 to honour Queen Charlotte, consort of George III. It became a town in 1855 and a city in 1875. The population is 17,063. It is the Island's single city.

The city's unofficial motto is "Cradle of Confederation," a reference to the important role played by the Islanders in hosting at Province House in 1864 one of the important pre-Confederation conferences. A plaque here marks the spot where the Fathers of Confederation "builded better than they knew." In a less sombre mood, when the future Prime Minister Sir John A. Macdonald signed the guestbook, he gave his occupation as "cabinet-maker."

The painter Robert Harris (1849-1919) was raised in Charlottetown; he is best remembered for his group portrait "The Fathers of Confederation," the original of which was lost in the fire on Parliament Hill of 1916. Born in Charlottetown was the once-popular novelist Basil King (1859-1928) who, five years before his death, told the Canadian Club of Toronto: "I imagine if I sold three copies of a book in Charlottetown in the course of three years, I am doing well."

Charlottetown is the capital of the Province of Prince Edward Island. To the Micmacs the island was known as Abegweit ("parallel to the shore"); to the French, Ile de Saint-Jean (1604); to the British, St. John's Island (1759) and Prince Edward Island (1798), after the Duke of Kent, father of Queen Victoria. The total population of the Island in 1983 was 123,600. The unofficial mottoes are "Garden of the Gulf," "Million Acre Farm," and "Spud Island."

CHICOUTIMI, Que.

On the south bank of the Saguenay River, about halfway between Lac Saint Jean and the St. Lawrence, is located Chicoutimi. The name derives from the Montagnais *shkoutimeou,* which means "the end of the deep water." A lumbering centre, Chicoutimi became a village in 1863, a town in 1879, and a city in 1930, with a population today of 135,172.

"I am in favour of equal rights for Canadians of French and English speech throughout Canada, within the limits of the practicable," said Eugene Forsey in 1961. "I am not in favour of insisting that every postal clerk in Vancouver should speak French, or every postal clerk in Chicoutimi English. They don't need to: there are not enough French-speaking people in Vancouver or English-speaking people in Chicoutimi."

Question: Which hockey player was known as "The Chicoutimi Cucumber"?

Answer: Georges Vézina (after his home town and his legendary coolness under pressure).

CONCEPTION BAY, Nfld.

Conception Bay, on the north shore of Newfoundland's Avalon Peninsula, is 12 miles (19 km) wide at the entrance and 28 miles (45 km) in extent. It includes smaller bays, among them Cupids Cove, the site of the first formal settlement on the island.

Folklore has it that Barren Island lies in Conception Bay. Leave it to the folklorists, as the toponomists have no record of such an island.

Conception Bay is one of the earliest of recorded names on the Atlantic coast. It was used in various forms in the early 1500s. Some English maps in the 1600s referred to it as Bay of Consumption.

Names in the Conception Bay area include: Blow Me Down Bluff, Burnt Stump, Ballyhack, Cupids, Pick Eyes, and Bareneed. Hibbs Hole, considered too indelicate, was officially changed to Hibbs Cove.

CORNER BROOK, Nfld.

Site of one of the world's largest paper mills and a centre for salmon fishing, Corner Brook was incorporated as a city in 1956. It is situated at the mouth of the Humber River on the west coast of the island. Corner Brook is Newfoundland's second-largest city, with a population of 32,269.

Pierre Juneau once claimed: "There are songs yet to be found in Sioux Lookout, Kamloops, Oromocto, Lévis, Corner Brook — wherever there are people."

No one who has read *House of Hate* (1970), an autobiographical novel by Percy Janes, will ever forget the author's description of life in his father's house in this mill town.

LAKE COUCHICHING, Ont.

There is no certainty about the meaning of the word Couchiching, which first appeared on a map in 1859 as *Cougichin,* identifying a stream that runs into the lake. It might well be an Indian word for "pinery" or "outlet." Of the two possibilities, "outlet" is the more appropriate, as the annual Couchiching Conference — an outlet for some — takes its name from Lake Couchiching which extends north from Lake Simcoe. Summer conferences have been held here since 1932 and winter conferences since 1954 under the sponsorship of the Canadian Institute on Public Affairs "to provide an open forum for discussion of Canadian social and economic problems in international settings." The conference centre, called Geneva Park — a name redolent of the League of Nations — is located 9 miles (14 km) north of Orillia, the summer home of Stephen Leacock (who could have mocked the thinkers' conferences, had he so decided). A writer who tackled the theme is the Hungarian-born intellectual and novelist, Stephen Vizinczey, who set a section of his episodic novel *In Praise of Older Women* (1965) at Geneva Park during "Couch." According to Vizinczey, the summer session is a veritable orgy.

CRAIGELLACHIE, B.C.

It is not by chance that the historic spot on the CPR line where the Last Spike was driven home bears the name Craigellachie. No doubt the coolies who laboured to complete the railroad experienced some difficulties pronouncing the Scots word. It was chosen by the CPR's General Manager, William Van Horne, when he learned that what had sustained the financier Donald A. Smith in his eleventh-hour fundraising on behalf of the bedevilled railroad were powerful childhood memories of Craigellachie — a massive rock near Banffshire, Scotland, and the clan rallying cry, "Stand fast, Craigellachie!" Indeed, this was the wording of Sir George Stephen's celebrated telegram to Smith — stand fast, and stand fast he did. Today, at Craigellachie, stands a plaque which reads in part: "A nebulous dream was a reality; an iron ribbon crossed Canada from sea to sea." The brief ceremony to mark the comple-

tion of the railway consisted of Smith driving home the Last Spike at 9:22 a.m., November 7, 1885, and a reassurance from Van Horne: "All I can say is that the work has been well done in every way." Suitably, the final nail was not a spike of gold but, like all the rest, of iron.

DARTMOUTH, N.S.

Named after the Earl of Dartmouth, who died in 1750, the year the settlement situated opposite Halifax on the east side of the harbour on the south coast of Nova Scotia was founded, Dartmouth became a town in 1873 and a city in 1961. It is linked with Halifax by a ferry system and two bridges and has a population of 62,277.

Dartmouth has been called the "city of lakes," for it has twenty-six. The abundance here of both fresh and salt water brings to mind the statement (made by the editors of the *Canada Year Book)* that "there are probably more lakes in Canada than in any other country." Water covers more than 70% of the earth's surface, yet even with all its surface water, only 7.6% of Canada is covered by fresh water. So the presence of fresh water is a valuable natural gift.

DAWSON, Y.T.

When it boasted a population of 25,000, it was called Dawson City. These days, with a population of 697, it is known as Dawson. Without question it is the country's — and perhaps the continent's — most celebrated "ghost town."

Dawson, on the east bank of the Yukon River at the confluence of the Klondike River, came alive in 1896 with the discovery of gold at nearby Bonanza Creek. Then, as abruptly as it had begun, the Klondike Gold Rush was over, the Trail of '98 was all but deserted by prospectors, and Dawson dwindled and diminished. It was the capital of the Yukon Territory from 1898 to 1953 when it yielded to Whitehorse. The city was named after George M. Dawson who directed the Geological Survey from 1895 to 1901.

Pierre Berton, who was born in the Yukon, catches the excitement of time and place in *City of Gold* (1957), an NFB short. An ill-advised attempt of the federal government to bolster tourism in the Yukon took the form of a summer festival of the arts in 1962. Bert Lahr starred in the world-premiere of the musical *Foxy*, base on Jonson's *Volpone*. Lahr refused to fly and took a series of trains and ships to and from Dawson. "Some of the cast cried when they first saw Dawson City, and we *all* cried when we left. The townspeople cried and the cast cried. It was sad."

DILDO, Nfld.

Perhaps the most astonishing of Canada's place names is Newfoundland's Dildo. It is as unexpected as it is direct. William B. Hamilton writes: "Of obscure derivation. The theories of origin include: 'a word used in the refrain of ballads'; 'a cylindrical glass'; 'phallus or penis substitute'; 'a local form of the doldrums.'"

Dildo is a village west of Bay Roberts in the Avalon Peninsula. There are numerous Dildos: in addition to the village, there are Dildo Arm, Dildo Cove, Dildo Islands, Dildo Pond, Dildo Run, and Dildo South.

Nearby will be found such features as: Spread Eagle Bay, Tickle Bay, Broad Cove, Heart's Delight, Heart's Desire, Fitters Cove, and Breakheart Point.

EDMONTON, Alta.

Edmonton is sometimes referred to as "The Gateway to the North," being the most northerly of Canada's major cities. (It occupies the same latitude as Liverpool and Hamburg.) It is situated on both banks of the North Saskatchewan River in almost the exact centre of the province. Fort Edmonton was established in 1801, the town in 1892, the city in 1904. The population is 657,057.

Edmontonians pride themselves on their parkland and on their city being "the oil capital of Canada." The site was named Edmonton by an HBC clerk in honour of his birthplace, now part of Metropolitan London, so the connection is slight indeed with Elizabeth Sawyer, who was hanged at Tyburn in 1621 and "immortalized" by Dekker, Ford, and Rowley as the woman who sells

her soul to the devil for the purposes of revenge in *The Witch of Edmonton,* the tragi-comedy first performed in London in 1623.

Edmonton has been the capital of the Province of Alberta since its formation in 1905. The Governor General the Marquess of Lorne named the district in honour of his wife Princess Louise Caroline Alberta, daughter of Queen Victoria. The population of the province in 1983 was 2,340,600. Who knows whether or not Allan Fotheringham was right in 1976 when he wrote: "The key to understanding Alberta is androgen, the male sex hormone, and the aura it projects, the insecurities it hides, the locker-room mentality it bolsters, explains the new rich kid on the block — the province of cowboys and *nouveau-riche* swagger."

FLIN FLON, Man.

Flin Flon is the only place in the world named after the hero of a dime novel. A mining community that straddles the Manitoba-Saskatchewan border, Flin Flon was founded in 1913, became a town in 1939, and boasts a present population of 9,897.

The dime novel is *The Sunless City* (1905), by J.E. Preston-Muddock, which describes how an English scientist, Professor Josiah Flintabbatey Flonatin, in a one-man submarine of his own design, descends through a tarn in the Rocky Mountains to the centre of the earth. Here he finds a kingdom where everything is laden with gold, where the inhabitants have tails, and where the females rule the males. After incredible adventures, the Professor (who is nicknamed Flin Flon) makes good his escape.

A copy of this fantastic adventure novel was found about 1913 at Churchill, 180 miles (288 km) north of the town, by Tom Creighton. Later, while prospecting in the area, Creighton plunged through the ice of the lake and, taking refuge in a rocky crevasse nearby, found a vein of gold. He identified the lake with Flin Flon's and gave the site its present name.

There is a dog-eared copy of the novel in the Flin Flon Public Library, and outside the town there stands a twenty-four-foot high statue of the eponymous hero. It was designed by the cartoonist Al Capp and erected in 1962 to draw attention to the Professor and to celebrate the 50th anniversary of northern Manitoba joining the southern part of the province.

FORT CHIMO, Que.

This tiny community began in 1830 on the bank of the Koksoak River near its outlet in Ungava Bay in Northern Quebec as an HBC post. It has a post office, an RCMP detachment, a health centre, a radio and weather station, and missions. Nearby is the government-run musk-ox farm at Umingmaqautik.

Chimo is a mixed Indian and Eskimo word of salutation. It is pronounced either "chee-mo" or "chy-mo." It means "greetings," though it is sometimes used as a toast (in place of "cheers").

Chimo!

P.S. It has just been learned that the official name of Fort Chimo is now Kuujuak. *Chimo* anyway!

FREDERICTON, N.B.

Originally an Acadian settlement called Sainte-Anne, the site was settled by early Loyalists and called St. Anne's Point. With the arrival of the Loyalists in 1785, it was named Fredericktown after HRH Prince Frederick, Bishop of Osnaburg. (The "k"and "w" were dropped shortly thereafter.) Fredericton, on both banks of the picturesque Saint John River, was incorporated as a city in 1848 and has a present population of 64,439.

One will not venture very far in Fredericton, or elsewhere in the province, without encountering evidences of "The Beaver." Max Aitken, the future lord Beaverbrook, was raised and educated in Newcastle and the Miramichi. He coveted the title of Lord Miramichi, but Louise Manny of Newcastle cautioned him by saying he would be called "Lord Merry Mickey"!

He was especially generous to the city of Fredericton, which boasts The Beaverbrook Art Gallery (with Jacob Epstein's bust of The Beaver), The Playhouse, Beaverbrookiana in the Harriet Irving Library, and such contributions to the University of New Brunswick as the Bonar Law-Bennett Building (home of the Provincial Archives and named after his friends), and a men's residence and gymnasium (named for Lady Beaverbrook). For the Beaver's remains, one must visit Newcastle, on the north shore, where his ashes are encased in a monument in the Square. He took his title not from Miramichi but from Beaver Brook Station, near

NTON

Newcastle. As John Buchan noted, "Beaverbrook was not a bad man: he is only a bad boy."

Fredericton is the capital of the Province of New Brunswick (the name of which honours King George III, a descendant of the House of Brunswick; it had originally been proposed to call it New Ireland). The province had a population in 1983 of 706,300.

FROBISHER BAY, N.W.T.

Located in the southern part of Baffin Island, Frobisher Bay is a town with a population of 2,333. Sir Martin Frobisher discovered the bay in 1576 and thought it was a strait. Settlement dates from 1942 when the U.S. Air Force established its base here.

Prince Charles made a brief visit in 1970. Asked his impressions, he replied, "I like Frobisher. But it looks like the moon."

GASPÉ, Que.

The word Gaspé is Micmac for "end" or "extremity." It applies to a cape, bay, basin, town, and county in southeastern Quebec. Jacques Cartier claimed the Gaspe Peninsula for the King of France on July 24, 1534, by erecting a thirty-foot wooden cross. Four hundred years later, in 1934, the landing was commemorated with the erection of another thirty-foot cross, this one of granite. The peninsula is dotted with picturesque farming and fishing villages. The area of Gaspé has a population of 17,261.

Samuel de Champlain in 1607 named the most famous site of the Gaspé Peninsula: Percé Rock. This enormous, low limestone rock off the eastern tip of the peninsula attracts both birds (for it has been a bird sanctuary since 1919) and tourists.

GIMLI, Man.

In Scandinavian mythology, Gimli is (in the words of one encyclopedia) "the great hall of heaven whither the righteous will go to spend eternity." It is also the name of a town on the west shore of Lake Winnipeg with a present population of 1,550, plus 2,375 in the surrounding district. Gimli is the site of the first permanent Icelandic settlement in Canada in 1875, and it remains ;the largest Icelandic community outside Iceland.

A twenty-foot statue of a bearded Viking warrior stands on the shore of Lake Winnipeg; and in nearby Arnes, there is Walter Yarwood's imposing sculptural monument to the explorer Viljalmur Stefansson with an inscription in three languages. In Icelandic, French, and English it says (in Stefansson's words): "I know what I have experienced, and I know what it has meant to me."

GRAND PRÉ, N.S.

Near Minas Basin at the head of the Bay of Fundy is found Grand Pré National Historic Park. The large Acadian population which settled here was deported in 1755. Five years following the Expulsion, English planters began farming here. The French name means "great meadow" and is derived from the Micmac description *mskegoo-a-kakik* ("grass at its occurrence place").

Grand Pré is essentially a memorial to the Acadians. Outside the little Church of St. Charles, dedicated to their memory, stands the bronze statue to Evangeline, begun by the sculptor Philippe Hébert and completed by his son Henri in 1920. The young Evangeline is seen from one angle, the old Evangeline from another. Longfellow's narrative poem, *Evangeline: A Tale of Acadie* (1847), tells the sad story of Emmeline Labische, separated from her lover at the time of the Expulsion, who finally found him in Louisiana but engaged to another woman.

The elegiac air of Grand Pré is caught in Bliss Carman's most famous poem, "Low Tide on Grand Pré," published in his first book of the same name in 1893:

> The night has fallen, and the tide ...
> Now and again comes drifting home,
> Across these aching barrens wide,
> A sigh like driven wind or foam:
> In grief the flood is bursting home.

THE GREAT LAKES

The Great Lakes, the largest basin of fresh water in the world, separate Ontario from eight American States — Minnesota, Wisconsin, Illinois, Michigan, Indiana, Ohio, Pennsylvania, and New York. It is easy to remember the names of the five lakes by recalling the mnemonic HOMES — Huron, Ontario, Michigan, Erie, and Superior.

Georgian Bay is sometimes described as "the sixth Great Lake." The five were first collectively described as "these great lakes" by Pierre-Esprit Radisson in 1665. Jay Gourlay, in *The Great Lakes Triangle* (1977), calls them "deadlier than the Bermuda Triangle."

"There is a quiet horror about the Great Lakes which grows as one revisits them," claimed Rudyard Kipling on his second trip across the country in 1908. To Rupert Brooke, writing in 1913, "A river and a little lake and an ocean are natural; but not these creatures. They are too big, and too smooth, and too sunny; like an American businessman."

Question: Which is the scariest lake in Canada?
Answer: Lake Erie.

HALIFAX, N.S.

"And Halifax, more than most towns, seemed governed by a fate she neither made nor understood, for it was her birthright to serve the English in time of war and to sleep neglected when there was peace. It was a bondage Halifax had no thought of escaping because it was the only life she had ever know ... the town figured more largely in the calamities of the British Empire than in its prosperities, and never seemed able to become truly North American."

So wrote Hugh MacLennan of this historic city in *Barometer Rising* (1941). It was founded in 1749 as a fortified British settlement (called Chebucto by the Micmacs) on the western shore of one of the world's finest harbours. It was named for George Montagu Dunk, Earl of Halifax, and became a town in 1841 and a city in 1848. The present population is 277,727. Like MacLennan, Rudyard Kipling caught the sad remoteness of Halifax in "The Song of the Cities" from *The Seven Seas* (1896):

Into the mist my guardian prows put forth,
  Behind the mist my virgin ramparts lie,
The Warden of the Honour of the North,
  Sleepless and veiled am I.

Halifax is the capital of the Province of Nova Scotia, which was as early as 1524 known as Acadia, the classical name for a land of pastoral peace. The name was conferred by the explorer Verrazano. Nova Scotia embraces both the mainland and Cape Breton Island, which is among the oldest names on the Atlantic seaboard, of Basque or Breton origin. The province's population in 1983 was 857,100.

HAMILTON, Ont.

Founded in 1813 at the foot of the Niagara Escarpment at the west end of Lake Ontario, Hamilton was originally known as Burlington Bay. It was given the name Hamilton in 1813 by the merchant Robert Hamilton to honour his son George; to honour his wife Catharine, he named St. Catharines, Ont. Hamilton became a town in 1833 and a city in 1846. The population is 542,095.

The iron and steel plants of Stelco and Dofasco have given the city the nickname "Steel City." (The motto of the latter is unforgettable: "Our product is steel. Our strength is people.") It has been called "the Pittsburgh of Canada." It is the country's third-largest industrial centre.

The well-known photographer John Reeves was born in the city, as were Karen Kain and Sylvia Fraser. Reeves made this intriguing observation about his home town: "Hamilton has an imaginary, Bergmany quality. It is isolated and in darkness, but it is also very much unto itself. There is a fanciful romanticism to the city. Hamilton has an exotic strain. You either become very much like it, and carry a lunch bucket, or you become its very antithesis, a fairy princess. Like Sylvia Fraser."

HUDSON BAY

Hudson Bay has been described as "one of the most distinctive and predominant water features on the entire planet when viewed from space." It is properly a "bay" of neither the Arctic Ocean nor the Atlantic Ocean but rather an "inland sea" in its own right.

It was discovered by the English navigator on his fourth and final voyage. On the night of June 23, 1611, his crew mutinied and Hudson, his son John, and seven faithful crew members were set adrift in a shallop near the mouth of the Rupert River in James Bay. Their fate has never been determined.

The drama of the episode was caught by Merrill Denison in the celebrated, stream-of-consciousness conclusion of the inaugural broadcast in the "Romance of Canada" radio series broadcast on January 22, 1931. Hudson is hallucinating: "See, my son... we're in mid-stream ... the boat's cast off the tow ... see above, our sails puff out their big white cheeks and we're away ... away, my son, away

IT'S HARD
NOT TO THINK
OF the Bay

again to seek the Western Passage. Look well at London Town and feast your eyes on those green English fields. See, yonder those good folks who wave to cheer us on our way. Look! There are cattle drinking by the stream. They, too, lift their heads and watch. And there is a shepherd with his flock. Look, lad, he waves his crook at us ... 'tis an omen, son ... God shepherds us above."

As David Thompson, the surveyor, wrote in 1784: "Hudson's Bay is certainly a country that Sinbad the Sailor never saw, as he makes no mention of mosquitoes."

The Geographic Board of Canada excised the apostrophe and the "s" in 1900, but the older designation lives on in the Hudson's Bay Company.

INUVIK, N.W.T.

Inuvik, on the Mackenzie River delta 100 miles (160 km) north of the Arctic Circle, was the first settlement designed and built for permanent residence in the Far North. It was established in 1955 to replace Aklavik as an administrative, transport, and service centre.

The Arctic explorer Sir Edward Parry wintered here in igloos in 1822-23. It is now a town of 3,147 with a post office, weather station, mission centre, RCMP detachment, and trading post, not to mention government offices. Inuvik means, in Inuktitut, "the place of man."

Vilhjalmur Stefansson addressed the question of Canada's slow acquisition of the North when he suggested that "the trouble lies in the fact that no prime minister has ever been exiled to the Arctic." Discussing John G. Diefenbaker's Northern Vision, historian John A. Munro found the North lacked appeal. "More important, it would seem that, apart from passing fits of romance, it was not the direction of enough Canadian dreams. Roads to Resources, the Pine Point Railway, mineral and glass exploration, the building of Inuvik were not sufficient to establish a northward pull. What was required was a northern miracle of major proportions to break the popular fixation with material and cultural goals established south of the 49th parallel. The creation of an industrial city of 75,000 people on the shores of Baffin Island might have done the job. This, and more's the pity, did not happen."

JOE BATT'S ARM, Nfld.

In any collection of Newfoundland place names, one of the most arresting entries has to be Joe Batt's Arm. This is the actual name of a town of 1,155 on the north shore of Fogo Island, 334 miles (534 km) north of St. John's. Charles Pedley, in his *The History of Newfoundland* (1863), is quoted by William B. Hamilton as saying it was named for Joe Batt "who was sentenced to receive fifteen lashes for stealing a pair of shoes and buckles valued at 7s 6p about 1754 at Bonavista." It should be borne in mind that "arm" is a nautical term for a passage of water, and is occasionally used to describe an arm-shaped projection of land.

KAMLOOPS, B.C.

Kamloops grew from a trading post established in 1812 at the confluence of the North and South Thompson rivers to a city, incorporated in 1893, with a population today of 64,997. The Indian name *kahm-o-loops* is said to mean "the meeting of the waters."

The name describes a game fish of varied size and colour found in the area. It has firm flesh and is excellent fresh or smoked. It usually inhabits inland lakes and streams and has been referred to as a landlocked Steelhead.

KANATA, Ont.

The Iroquois word *kanata* means a "community" or "collection of huts." It is the basis of the name Canada. Curiously, the word earliest associated with the history of the country is the word increasingly associated with the future of the country. Kanata is becoming synonymous with Canada's handhold on future technology.

Kanata is the name of a suburb of Ottawa, a municipality in Ottawa-Carleton established in the early 1960s with a present population of 19,728. As Val Sears wrote in 1982: "This is Ottawa's newest intellectual pulse, Silicon Valley, west of the city, the richest concentration of high-technology hustlers in all of Canada."

Here are located almost 250 firms employing 14,000 people in telecommunications, computers, and microtechnology. Canada's Silicon Valley? Inevitably Silicon Valley North.

KINGSTON, Ont.

Located on the north shore of Lake Ontario, where it empties into the St. Lawrence, halfway between Montreal and Toronto, Kingston is an historic city. Here the Iroquois established their Cataraqui ("place where one hides," "impregnable," "rocks drenched with water" — all are possible meanings). The French established Fort

Frontenac here in 1673; the English, King's Town in 1784. The settlement, named after King George III in 1788, became a town in 1838 and a city in 1846. The present population is 114,982.

Walt Whitman visited Kingston in 1880 and called it "a pretty town," reserving his enthusiasm for the Thousand Islands ("the most beautiful extensive region of lakes and islands one can probably see on earth"). Two years later, Oscar Wilde lectured on aesthetics in the Opera House. The lecture was sparsely attended, but Wilde was philosophical and quipped to a reporter: "Any man could speak well to a crowd, but it required a mighty effort to thrill empty benches."

Kingston figures as Salterton in three novels by Robertson Davies: *Tempest-Tost* (1951), *Leaven of Malice* (1954), and *A Mixture of Frailties* (1958).

KITCHENER, Ont.

Kitchener was called Sand Hill and Ebytown before it was named Berlin in 1824 in deference to its Pennsylvania-Dutch settlers from Pennsylvania and immigrants from Germany. It became a village in 1854, a town in 1870, and a city in 1912. Due to anti-German feeling during the War, the statue of the Kaiser in the park was dumped into the lake and replaced by that of Queen Victoria. In 1916, the name was changed to honour the British war leader, the late Lord Kitchener of Khartoum. It is located in southern Ontario between London and Toronto and has a population of 287,801.

Kitchener is celebrated for its Farmers' Market, its annual Oktoberfest, and Woodside, the boyhood home of Mackenzie King. In the 1950s, the city advertised itself as "Clean as a Kitchen." The phrase "Kit-Wat" is often used, for Kitchener is one half of the "Twin Cities," the other half being the adjoining community of Waterloo.

It was with Lord Kitchener that Sir Sam Hughes had his famous disagreement of 1914 about the division of Canadian troops. "You have your orders, carry them out," Kitchener barked. "I'll be damned if I will," Sir Sam replied, turning on his heel and marching out of the office.

KLONDIKE, Y.T.

This region in the west central part of the Yukon Territory includes the Klondike River and its tributary, Bonanza Creek, scene of the famous Klondike Gold Rush of 1896. The name is derived from the Kutchin word for the Klondike River — "hammer creek" — and identifies, in addition to a region and a river, a village, a range of hills, and a plateau.

Two sobriquets: Klondike Mike refers to a colourful character named Michael Mahoney who carried a grand piano over the White

Pass in 1898. King of the Klondike applies to Joseph W. Boyle, prospector and adventurer, who founded a gold-dredging operation in the North, then engaged in espionage activities in Europe during the First World War.

"The Klondike experience had taught all these men that they were capable of a kind of achievement they had never dreamed possible," explained Pierre Berton in his book *Klondike* (1958).

Set in neighbouring Alaska but based on the experiences of countless prospectors is *The Gold Rush,* the feature-length silent film released in 1925 starring Charles Chaplin.

L'ANSE AUX MEADOWS, Nfld.

A remote fishing village adjacent to the Strait of Belle Isle on the northeast tip of the Island of Newfoundland, L'Anse aux Meadows was found to be, in the summer of 1960, the site of the first indisputable Norse settlement uncovered in North America. House-sites plus other archaeological remains were scientifically dated to about A.D. 1000, which corresponds to dates of occupation suggested by the *Greenlander's Saga* and other narratives in Old Norse. On the strength of such evidence, Helge Ingstad identified the outport with Vinland, the Norse colony founded by the Greenlander Leif Ericsson (called The Lucky). Further work equated Helluland with Cape Dyer on Baffin Island, and Markland with Cape Porcupine in Labrador. The name L'Anse aux Meadows is part French and part English for "the bay of meadows," though it may also mean "the bay of jellyfish" (*L'Anse aux Meduses*). Newfoundlanders pronounce the place name "Lancy Meadows."

It was once popularly held that Vikings had settled in northern Ontario and in Minnesota. In 1930, a cache of authentic Norse weapons turned up near Beardmore in the Lake Nipigon area and were bought by the Royal Ontario Museum which exhibited them for some years as artifacts. Now ROM will not even release photographs of them. Throughout the 1930s, James W. Curran, the publicity-minded publisher of the Sault Ste. Marie *Daily Star,* maintained that "a Norseman died in Ontario 900 years ago" and in 1939 published a book on the subject.

Question: Who are the six kings of early Canada?
Answer: The VI Kings.

LETHBRIDGE, Alta.

Lethbridge in southern Alberta was named in 1885 for William Lethbridge, the president of a local coal company. Earlier, for fifteen or so years, the coal-mining community was known as Coalbanks. Lethbridge became a town in 1891 and a city in 1906. Farming and ranching now match mining as the main activities that support the population of 54,072.

Earlier this century, the natives of Lethbridge objected to the name Belly River, the official name for the tributary of the Bow River. They suggested Alberta River, but the authorities would not endorse the suggestion. Ultimately the solution was to make the Belly a tributary of Oldman River.

According to James H. Gray in *Red Lights on the Prairies* (1971). Lethbridge in the 1920s and 30s had the largest brothel in Western Canada. Today the city is widely known for Nikka Yuko, the largest Japanese garden in North America, which was built by the city and Japanese Canadians who had been relocated there during the Second World War. It includes a five-tiered pagoda with ceremonial bell and a turtle-shaped island in a pond.

LONDON. Ont.

"That's a piece of impertinence in itself!" exclaimed Brendan Behan in 1961 when told that there was a city in Ontario named after *the* London.

It was John Graves Simcoe's wish to establish his administrative centre here, on the banks of the Thames River, which the French had earlier called La Tranche. He renamed the river in 1792 and the following year called his settlement at "the Forks of the Thames" New London. The "New" was quickly dropped and while it never became the centre it was meant to be it did prosper. London became a town in 1848 and a city in 1855. The present population is 283,668. It is sometimes called "the Hartford of Canada," in reference to the head offices of insurance companies located here.

In the late 19th century, London was occasionally dubbed "London the Lesser." It is the birthplace of Hume Cronyn and Kate Nelligan and the home of Grand Theatre which was established here in 1983 by Robin Phillips.

LOUISBOURG, N.S.

The Louis of Louisbourg is the Sun King, Louis XIV, who ordered the construction in 1713 of this immense French fortress on the eastern tip of Cape Breton (then known as Ile-Royale). It housed some five thousand men and was the largest citadel in North America. Twice it fell to the English before it was demolished in 1760 by British sappers commanded by the father of the poet Lord Byron.

Today the Fortress is part of Louisbourg National Historic Park and the centre of a vast reconstruction project to return the buildings to their former, 17th-century glory. The town has a permanent population of 1,410; engaged in the reconstruction are archaeologists and architects, historians and scholars.

When Vauban the military architect approached Louis XV for further funds to complete Louisbourg, the King replied: "Are the streets being paved with gold over there? I fully expect to awake one morning in Versailles to see the walls of the fortress rising above the horizon." It is a vision worthy of the painter Magritte.

MANITOULIN ISLAND, Ont.

Manitoulin Island bears the name of the Manitou, the Algonkian "spirit" or "mystery." This island, in Lake Huron adjacent to northern Georgian Bay, has been occupied for 12,000 years. Today about 4,500 Indians live on the island, almost half its present population.

Manitoulin is world's largest freshwater island, with an area of 1,068 square miles (2,766 km^2). It may be the largest of freshwater islands, but it is nowhere near the size of Canada's largest saltwater islands, the largest of which are (in decreasing size): Baffin Island, Victoria Island, and Ellesmere Island. Baffin is 195,928 square miles (507,451 km^2).

Robert McMichael visited the Wikwemikong Reserve on Manitoulin Island in 1975 to examine the work of the Indian artist James Simon. McMichael was impressed; noting certain surreal touches to the canvases, he asked Simon if he was familiar with the work of Salvador Dali. "Salvador Dali?" replied the young artist. "I think I know that guy's name. What reservation is he on?"

MEDICINE HAT, Alta.

Medicine Hat is located in the southeastern part of Alberta, 170 miles (284 km) southeast of Calgary. It was named after the Blackfoot *saamis,* "the headdress of a medicine man," in 1894, the year it became a village. It achieved town status in 1898 and city status in 1906, with a present population of 49,645.

Stephen Leacock, not content with its location midway between Moose Jaw and Calgary, quipped that Medicine Hat is halfway between Peking and London. Rudyard Kipling, passing through in 1907, calling it "the town that was born lucky," said: "You people in this district seem to have all Hell for a basement" — an allusion to the natural gas in the area.

In 1910, some townsfolk agitated to give the city a more conventional name. Kipling sent a strong letter in support of retaining the original. "Believe me, the very name is an asset, and as years go on will become more and more an asset. It has the no duplicate in the world; it makes men ask questions ... it has the qualities of uniqueness, individuality, assertion, and power ... what, then, should a city be rechristened that has sold its name? Judasville."

The photographer Roloff Beny wrote in 1973: "Medicine Hat, an oasis in a deep valley carved by the serpentine South Saskatchewan, is where I didn't elect to be born."

MIRABEL, Que.

International airports have the comfortable habit of never completely shedding their traditional names. Thus, Montreal International Airport remains Dorval; Ottawa International Airport is known as Uplands; Toronto Interantional Airport persists as Malton, etc.

Montreal's second airport, the world's largest airport, and the first supersonic airport is Mirabel International Airport, which when it was opened in 1975 was designed to handle 10 million passengers in the first year (and 60 million annually by the year 2025). It is located northwest of the city in the displaced community of Sainte-Scholastique which dated back to 1825. The city of Mirabel was created in 1971 and named two years later. It now has a population of 14,080. The new airport is generally conceded to be a "white elephant," being much too large and distant from Montreal.

The name Mirabel is derived from a community name, which is said to come from a farm that was on the site; the farm was named after the farmer's two daughters, Miriam and Isabel. That at least is the lore.

MONCTON, N.B.

Transportation centre of the Maritimes, Moncton was originally called The Bend, after a bend in the Petitcodiac River on which it is situated, and then Monckton, after the English commander Robert Monckton who was wounded in the Battle of the Plains of Abraham. A clerk dropped the "k" in 1786 and it became Moncton (although in 1930 the letter was briefly restored). It became a town in 1855 and a city in 1890, with a present population of 98,354. One-third French, it is the largest urban centre of Acadie.

When Oscar Wilde made his lecture tour of Central and Eastern Canada in 1882, the only place to present problems was Moncton. Here the sheriff served him a writ, due to a disagreement between local sponsors. "The whole thing illustrates the illegality of most law and the immorality of most moral institutions," wrote Wilde when back in Boston. "Such associations are usually the refuge of the provincial Joseph Surfaces. True, it afforded me an interesting insight into certainly not a very favourable side of Canadian ordinary life, and for experience one would go through a great deal, even to a sudden visit from the sheriff."

Just northwest of the city centre is the justly famous "Magnetic Hill," where a car driven to the "bottom" of the hill will appear to coast "up" the hill. Known locally from the 1920s, it first attracted wide attention in 1933 when made the subject of articles by Stuart Trueman and other writers.

MONTREAL, Que.

Montreal is the world's second-largest, French-speaking city (after Paris) and the second most-populous in Canada (after Toronto). The city is dominated by Mount Royal, an extinct volcano 764 feet (1,222 km) high; atop Mount Royal is a giant, illuminated cross visible up to 50 miles (80 km).

In 1535, Jacques Cartier climbed and named "le Mont Ruiall." Ville-Marie de Montréal was founded in 1642, termed Montréal in 1724, established as a town in 1792 and as a city in 1832. The population is 2,828,349, and predominantly French, for Montreal

is the centre of Québécois culture and commerce. Perhaps Brendan Behan had *joual* or racial rivalry in mind when he quipped: "Montreal is the only place where a good French accent isn't a social asset."

Mark Twain lived in Montreal for six months in 1881. "What you lack in weather you make up in the means of grace," he said at a banquet in his honour at the Windsor Hotel. "This is the first time I was ever in a city where you couldn't throw a brick without breaking a church window. Yet I was told that you were going to build one more. I said the scheme is good, but where are you going to find room? They said, we will build it on top of another church and use an elevator. This showed that the gift of lying is not yet dead in the land."

The novelist Hugh MacLennan, who has pondered the mysteries of the city, wrote in his novel *The Watch that Ends the Night* (1958): "A wise woman said to me not long ago that Montreal's real character is reflected in the faces of the women of its older families, so many of whom, even if not beautiful, contrive to give that illusion of beauty which comes to a woman who knows she has been admired, perhaps even loved, by more than one man, yet is discreet, guarding her own enrichment. The silence of Montreal people about the things that matter most to them is not really hypocritical; it is a protection of the quiet and deliberately chosen intricacy of their lives."

MOOSE JAW, Sask.

Moose Jaw lies on the CP line midway between the province's borders with Alberta and Manitoba; it is also halfway between Calgary and Winnipeg. It was settled in 1882, became a town in 1884 and a city in 1903. The population is 36,057. The name Moose Jaw Creek is recorded on a map in 1857; the creek in question makes a more than 90-degree turn, said to give it the configuration of a moose's jawbone.

On the Prairies one is always aware of the transitoriness of the things of man. As Edward McCourt wrote in *The Road across Canada* (1965): "Troy town rose and fell ten times on the hill Hissarlik above the Hellespont; the Indian village sited a few miles west of Moose Jaw went Troy three better — thirteen distinct cultural levels have been uncovered in the Mortlach 'midden,' first stumbled upon by a local farmer who observed an unusual number of arrowheads in a pasture cowpath."

Art Linkletter, of "People are Funny" fame, was born in Moose Jaw in 1912. Earl Cameron, CBC-TV newscaster, was born here three years later.

In 1983, the Mayor of Moose Jaw, Louis H. (Scoop) Leury, announced that the city would acquire an immense concrete-and-steel moose, sculpted by Don Foulds. "It'll be a great moose. There'll be nothing like it anywhere. It'll be 18 feet high at the withers, 30 feet at the antlers. People will come from all over to see it." Apparently the Moose Jaw moose will be call Mac.

MOUNT LOGAN, Y.T.

Mount Logan is the highest mountain in Canada, and after Alaska's Mount McKinley, the highest in North America. It is the peak of peaks in the mighty St. Elias Mountains, being 19,523 feet (5,951 m) above sea level. In comparison, the world's highest mountain, Everest in Asia, is almost 10,000 feet (3,040 m) higher than Mount Logan. And to place Everest in perspective, the highest peak known to man is Olympus Mons which is 88,560 feet (27,000 m) in height. (Olympus Mons on Mars is the largest volcano in the solar system.)

Mount Logan may be massive but it is somewhat featureless. It is the centrepiece of Kluane National Park Reserve. Its name honours William Logan, founder of the Geological Survey of Canada. Mount Logan was first climbed to its snowy peak in 1925.

Interviewed on the set of *Niagara,* the movie star Marilyn Monroe said: "When they said Canada, I thought it would be up in the mountains somewhere."

Ed Ogle, bureau chief of *Time* in 1958, interviewed a retired Saskatchewan farmer who had taken up residence in Kelowna, B.C., and asked him if he enjoyed the Okanagan Valley. "The mountains are all right, I guess, but they sure do block the view."

NAHANNI NATIONAL PARK, N.W.T.

The meaning of Nahanni in the language of the Slavey Indians is "people of the west." The name now refers to a butte, a mountain, a range, two rivers, a place (population 90), and a park in the southwest part of the Northwest Territories. The North Nahanni River is a tributary of the Mackenzie. The South Nahanni River, a tributary of the Liard, flows through rugged Nahanni National Park, which was officially opened in 1972.

Legends emanate from the valley of the South Nahanni — legends of lost mines, hot springs, tropical foliage, strange tribes (ruled over by a "white queen"), prehistoric beasts, apertures to unknown worlds, etc. Through this region runs the Sick Heart River, a wild riverway unknown to cartographers, the valley of which possesses strange properties. As John Buchan wrote in *Sick Heart River* (1941): "There was no place for life in it — there could not be; but neither was there room for death. This peace was beyond living and dying .... "

NANAIMO, B.C.

Nanaimo is on the east coast of Vancouver Island across the Strait of Georgia from Vancouver. An HBC fort was built here in 1853, the settlement was named in 1860, and the city was incorporated in 1874. It has a population of 57,694.

The name Nanaimo is said to be Indian (*sne-ny-mo,* "big strong people") after the confederation of tribes here. To the south is Petroglyph Provincial Park where there are stylized carvings on rock of humans, birds, animals, and strange creature, in addition to parallel lines as long as 40 feet (12 km).

NEW WESTMINSTER, B.C.

Located on the north bank of the Fraser River about 20 miles (32 km) from its mouth, New Westminster is the largest freshwater port on the Pacific coast of Canada. Named by Queen Victoria after *the* Westminster in 1858, it served as the British Columbian capital from 1860 to 1886 when the provincial seat was transferred to Victoria. The Royal City (as it is still called) has a population of 38,550.

Newspaper columnist Barry Mather adapted a piece of popular lore when he said: "A British Columbian is a man who has a California-style house, a Montreal mortgage, an English car, and a Scottish dog. His wife, who comes from Regina or maybe it is Calgary, either has a cat whose forbears came from Persia or a small bird from the tropics which she keeps in a cage allegedly imported from Eastern Canada, but more likely made in Japan."

NIAGARA FALLS, Ont.

Niagara Falls may not be the highest waterfall in the world (Angel Falls in Venezuela has that honour, being 17 times higher), or even the highest in Canada (Takakkaw Falls in British Columbia takes the honour, being 8 times higher), but it is certainly the most famous cataract of all time. Indeed, the city of Niagara Falls advertises itself as "The World's Most Famous Address" and "The Honeymoon Capital of the World."

Early names for the settlements here are Elgin, Clifton, and Drummondville. As a place name, Niagara Falls was introduced in 1881, and the town acquired city status in 1904. The population today is 70,960.

Niagara is said to mean, in Huron, "thunder of waters." There is even the suggestion that this is the last surviving word of the language spoken by the long-extinct Neutral Nation. The Falls were first described in 1678 by the missionary Louis Hennepin, who overestimated the height by three. The American Fall is 167 feet high (50 m), the Canadian (or Horseshoe) Fall 162 feet high (48 m). Since that first description, exaggeration has been an essential part of the Falls experience.

To Oscar Wilde, who viewed them in 1882, they were ludicrous. He observed, "Niagara Falls must be the second major disappointment of American married life." Yet the following year, to the novelist Henry James, they appeared in all their aesthetic glory. "You can only stand there gazing your fill at the most beautiful object in the world."

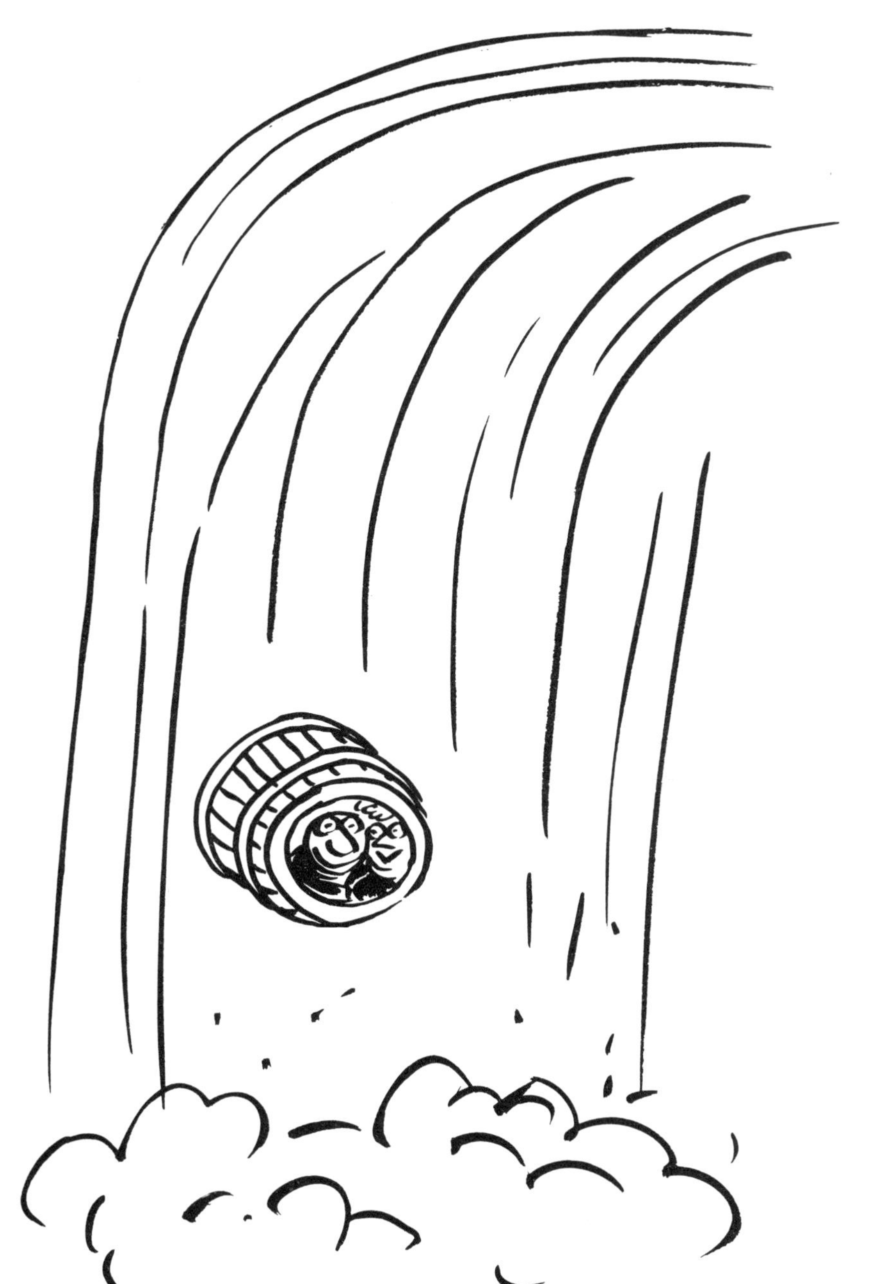

NORANDA, Que.

Noranda is a mining city in the Abitibi region close to the Ontario border. With the discovery of ore deposits here in 1911, the Noranda Mines were opened. The town was incorporated in 1926 and acquired city status in 1948. The population is 8,767. Its twin city, Rouyn, was named after Captain de Rouyn, an officer in Montcalm's army.

Noranda is an acronym, being made up of letters from the two words *Nor*th *Canada*. Such playful, portmanteau place names dot the country. They are relatively rare in Atlantic Canada, but quite frequent in Western Canada. Here are some not otherwise included in this collection:

Alcan Highway, Y.T. (*Al*aska, *Can*ada); Castlegar, B.C. (*Castle Gar*dens); Elkford, B.C. (*Elk* River, *Ford*ing River); Lake Koocanusa, B.C. (*Koo*tenay, *Can*ada, *USA);* Tadanac, B.C. (*T*rail, *Canada* backwards); Hemaruka, Alta. (*He*len, *Mar*y, *Ru*th, *Ka*thleen); Canora, Sask. (*Can*adian *Nor*thern *Ra*ilway); Estevan, Sask. (Georg*e Ste*phen, W.C. *Van* Horne); Kerrobert, Sask. (R*obert Kerr);* Transcona (*trans*continental, Lord Strath*cona);* Kenora, Ont. (*Ke*ewatin, *Nor*man, *Ra*t Portage); Quetico, Ont. (*Que*bec *Ti*mber *Co*mpany); Walden, Ont. (*Wa*ters, *L*ively, *Den*ison); Arvida, Que. (*Ar*thur *Vi*ning *Da*vis). Etc. (*Et C*etera.)

THE NORTH POLE

"There is no spot on the face of the earth which has given rise to so many hypotheses and chimeras," wrote Jules Verne of the High Arctic and the Polar Region. Some men are possessed by "the polar passion," according to Farley Mowat. Canada, being a circumpolar country, has claims on both Poles.

"All compasses point to Canada," someone once said. In 1831, the Arctic explorer James Ross discovered that they were pointing to Boothia Peninsula where the north pole of the earth's magnetic field was then located. But the North Magnetic Pole "wanders" — often by as much as 200 miles (320 km) in a few decades — and is presently located on Bathurst Island in the Northwest Territories. So all compasses point a little north of Bathurst Island's Erskine Inlet.

"No...
This is The
MAGNETIC
North
Pole..."

The North Pole proper, that is, the North Geographic Pole, is the northern point of the earth's rotation on its axis. The point is situated in a polar ice cap north of Ellesmere Island. The North Pole was first "attained" by two claimants: Frederick A. Cook on April 21, 1908, and/or Robert E. Peary with Mathew Henson on April 6, 1909.

Superman's Fortress of Solitude is located at the North Pole, and so is Santa's Castle. Here Santa Claus lives and works with his elves making toys for little boys and girls. In the pre-Christmas season, Canada Post replies to letters addressed to: Santa Claus, North Pole, Canada, H0H 0H0.

OKANAGAN VALLEY, B.C.

This fruit-farming valley is located in the interior of British Columbia. The possible meaning of the Salishan word from which

Okanagan was derived is "top" or "head," in reference to a point in the Okanagan River. Kelowna is the largest city, incorporated in 1905, with a present population of 59,196. (Kelowna means "grizzly bear.") Penticton (meaning "the always place"), incorporated in 1948, has a population of 23,181.

Lake Okanagan is celebrated as the habitat of Ogopogo, the fabulous sea serpent sighted regularly each spring by residents and tourists alike. The monster's name is said to derive from an old music hall song or from the Shushwap name for the creature of the depths, variously described as snake-like, prehistoric-looking, etc. Ogopogo is a palindrome — a word which reads the same backward or forward.

Two Inuit words in common use are palindromic: *kayak* (a one-man canoe) and *ulu* (a woman's knife; also the name of a mountain). Communities with palindromes for names include Glenelg (near Guysborough, N.S.), Laval (near Quebec City, Que.), Navan (near Ottawa, Ont.), and Wakaw (near Prince Albert, Sask.). Three Ontario townships are palindromal: Oro (near Barrie), Oso (near Sharbot Lake), and Otto (near Kirkland Lake).

OLD CROW, Y.T.

Located some 70 miles (112 km) north of the Arctic Circle, near the Alaska border, Old Crow is the most northern settlement in the Yukon. Its name honours Walking Crow *(Te-Tahim-Gevtik)*, a Loucheux chief who died in the 1870s. Since 1926, Old Crow has had a post office, an RCMP detachment, and a mission. The population is 221.

The most celebrated citizen of Old Crow has to be Edith Josie, the Loucheux correspondent, whose vivid (though ungrammatical) columns appear in the *Whitehorse Star*. A collection, *The Best of Edith Josie*, was published in 1963. One of her columns might begin "Here are the news" and continue: "It is the very small village here at Old Crow but the news is getting better every week. I'm sure glad that everyone gets my news and know every thing what people are doing." A column will usually conclude: "This is end the news."

ORILLIA, Ont.

The mellifluous name Orillia may be derived from Spanish or Indian words. The township was named in 1820 by Lieutenant-Governor Sir Peregrine Maitland (who had formerly served in Spain). *Orilla* is Spanish for "river bank." *Orelia* is said to be Algonkian for "red berries," but this may be coincidental. Orillia, formerly The Narrows, then Newton, became a village in 1867 and a town in 1875 with a present population of 30,860.

Mariposa is Sir Peregrine's name for a township in Victoria County, and it means "butterfly" in Spanish. It is also the name given by Stephen Leacock to an Orillia-like town in his celebrated book *Sunshine Sketches of a Little Town* (1912). Leacock was raised in the region and had his summer home (now a tourist attraction) on Old Brewery Bay, Lake Couchiching.

"Mariposa is not a real town," wrote Leacock. "On the contrary, it is about seventy or eighty of them. You may find them all the way from Lake Superior to the sea, with the same square streets and the same maple trees and the same churches and hotels, and everywhere the sunshine of the land of hope."

OSHAWA, Ont.

Oshawa has been called "The Go Ahead City" and "The Detroit of Canada" (for the McLaughlin-Buick and the General Motors works). The settlement goes back to Skae's Corners in 1794. The name Oshawa dates from 1842 and is Seneca for "carrying place." A village in 1850, a town in 1879, and a city in 1924, it has a population today of 154, 217.

Two attractions of the city are Parkwood, Colonel Sam McLaughlin's estate, and the Canadian Automotive Museum. James Bond learned his tricks near Oshawa. It seems the author Ian Fleming trained in espionage work at Camp X, a top-secret training camp which operated during the Second World War under the direction of Sir William Stephenson, renowned as "The Quiet Canadian" and "Intrepid."

The classic observation concerning Oshawa has to be the Happy Hooker's. When Xaviera Hollander was promoting one of her bestselling books in Oshawa, she asked a rhetorical question, then answered it. "You know what I think Oshawa needs? A good brothel."

❦ OTTAWA, Ont.

Ottawa takes its name from the Algonkian word *adawe,* which means "to trade" or "to barter." The etymology is appropriate for a power-broker city. In French, the Ottawa River is known as Rivière des Outaouais, and the region around Hull, Aylmer, and Gatineau is called the Outaouais.

The nation's capital was originally called Bytown, after Colonel John By of the Royal Engineers who built the Rideau Canal in 1826-32. It became a town in 1847 and a city in 1855 when it acquired its present name. The combined population of the Ottawa-Hull region (as the National Capital Commission has persisted in designating the area since 1974) is 717,978. The Ontario portion, the Regional Municipality of Ottawa-Carleton is 547,399; the Quebec portion, the Outaouais Region, 170,579. Ottawa has been a capital city since 1857 and capital of Canada since Confederation in 1867.

When Oscar Wilde lectured on aesthetics in Ottawa in 1882, he admired the scenery around the city but condemned the sawdust pollution on the Ottawa River. "This is an outrage; no one has a right to pollute the air and water, which are the common inheritance of all; we should leave them to our children as we have received them." A little later the political analyst Goldwin Smith wrote, "Ottawa is a sub-arctic lumber-village converted by royal mandate into a political cockpit."

Rupert Brooke toured the country in 1913 and observed: "The Indians have passed. They left no arts, no tradition, no buildings or roads or laws; only a story or two, and a few names, strange and beautiful. The ghosts of the old chiefs must surely chuckle when they note that the name by which Canada has called her capital and the centre of her political life, Ottawa, is an Indian name which signifies 'buying and selling.'"

No Canadian, whether native or new, succeeds in shucking off the intimations of sentiment and nostalgia occasioned by viewing the Peace Tower, Rideau Hall, the National War Memorial, etc. Brooke saw and heard in Ottawa "a barely materialized national spirit ... and the rather lovely sound of the soft Canadian accent in the streets". Contemporary writers are more inclined to parry with wit, as Allan Fotheringham did in 1972: "Ottawa? Well, it's sort of a provincial Washington. That's it. That's it. Yesterday's city tomorrow!"

PANGNIRTUNG, N.W.T.

Pangnirtung is Inuktitut for "place of the bull caribou." Pang (as it is called) commands a view of Cumberland Sound in the eastern part of Baffin Island. The hamlet of 839 dates back to 1921 and includes a mission church, post office, trading post, weather station, and RCMP unit.

Life has changed profoundly for the Inuit of Pang, as the nomadic life has been replaced by the more sedentary life. There is a sadness and a sameness to most of the statements made by elderly Inuit in *Stories from Pangnirtung* (1976), illustrated by Germaine Arnaktauyok, As Josephee Sowdloapik, a former hunter of bull caribou, sixty-five, concluded his narrative: "This is the end of my stories, and all of them are true. I used to be a brave man."

PEGGYS COVE

Some places are "as pretty as a picture," and this fishing village about 25 miles (40 km) southwest of Halifax is one of them. For years the brightly painted houses, the weather-beaten coast, the rocky terrain, and the snug harbour have attracted painters and photographers. No one is certain when the village was founded or how many live here year round. Peggys Cove might have been named after the wife of William Rodgers, an early settler, or it might have acquired its name from St. Margarets Bay on which it is situated. Peggys Cove is among the most picturesque of spots in the country.

POVUNGNITUK, Que.

Povungnituk — or Pov, for short — has a mission and trading post and it does go back to 1927. The present population is 681. It is located on the east side of Hudson Bay at the mouth of the Povungnituk River. Would it be a pleasant place to visit? Perhaps the original Inuktitut meaning of the word answers that question. Povungnituk means "place of bad smells."

PRINCE ALBERT, Sask.

Prince Albert was named after the German-born consort of Queen Victoria. The Victoria and Albert Museum in Ottawa and the Albert Hall in London, England, also bear his name.

Prince Albert, which was named in 1866, is located in the epicentre of Saskatchewan. It became a town in 1885 and a city in 1904. This farming and lumber centre, with a population of 38,331, has the distinction of having elected three prime ministers — Sir Wilfrid Laurier, W.L. Mackenzie King, and John G. Diefenbaker. The latter, who lived in the riding, and failed to be elected the city's mayor, liked to boast: "As Prince Albert goes, so goes the nation."

PRINCE GEORGE, B.C.

This city bears the name of George III, the British king who "lost" the American Colonies in 1776. He was the first sovereign of his house to speak English from birth, and the grandfather of Queen Victoria.

Sir Alexander Mackenzie, on his celebrated trek in 1793 across the country, passed by the future site of Prince George. Simmon Fraser established a NWC post here, and the site was known as Fort George until 1915 when it became a city with its present name. There are 59,929 residents in this city, located in the virtual geographic centre of British Columbia.

PUGWASH, N.S.

When a reporter asked Cyrus Eaton the location of Pugwash, the industrialist replied, "Why, good heavens, man! Pugwash is right there between Shinimicas and Tatamagouche!"

The millionaire peace advocate was born in Pugwash, a small fishing village on an inlet of Northumberland Strait, east of Amherst. The name comes from *Pagweak,* Micmac for "shallow water," although Eaton maintained the word meant "deep water." He arranged for Bertrand Russell to invite nuclear scientists from ten nations, including the U.S. and the U.S.S.R., to meet here and discuss world peace. Scientists have continued to meet under the Pugwash banner which was first unfurled in July 1957. Their deliberations have somewhat eased Cold War tensions and nuclear anxieties.

If the Pugwashians had not resisted the movement in 1826 to change their village's name from "its present uncouth name to Waterford," the First Pugwash Conference of Nuclear Scientists would have been called the First Waterford Conference of Nuclear Scientists.

PUNKEYDOODLES CORNERS, Ont.

This community southwest of Kitchener by 18 miles (28 km), where Waterloo County meets Perth County and Oxford County, is famous for its funny name. *The Gazetteer of Canada: Ontario* refers to it as a "dispersed rural community." The voters here are often questioned to determine trends in voting patterns in the country. In 1982, a reporter described Punkeydoodles Corners as consisting of fourteen inhabitants, three houses, and one barn. As for the peculiar name, it is said to derive from the pumpkins grown by the Swiss settler John Zurbrigg or from the mispronunciation of German hotel owner John Zurbuchen's "Yankee Doodle Went To Town."

PUNKEYDOODLES
POPULATION
dispersed

PUSH AND BE DAMNED RAPIDS, N.B.

There are two Push and Be Damned Rapids in New Brunswick, and none elsewhere. One is on the Southwest Miramichi River, Stanley Parish, York County; the other is on the Nepisiquit River, Bathurst Parish, Gloucester County. William B. Hamilton explains that the Push and Be Damned Narrows, on the Letang River, in St. George and Pennfield Parish, Charlotte County, were named in response to "the problems encountered in rowing against the on-rushing water."

QU'APPELLE RIVER, Sask.

The fort, two towns, and valley were all called after the Qu'Appelle River in southern Saskatchewan. The French name (it means "who calls") derives from the Cree *Kah-tep-was* ("the river which calls"). The town, east of Regina, was settled in 1882. It became a village in 1898 and a town in 1904. It now has a population of 653, the majority of whom are appreciative of Pauline Johnson's poem "The Legend of Qu'Appelle Valley" found in *Flint and Feather* (1912). The poem tells the legend of a young brave, who passing the valley on his way to his village hears his lover call out his name. He answers, "Qu'Appelle?" but there is only a maddening echo. Arriving home, he finds his fiancée dead. Yet she has called his name across the valley.

QUEBEC CITY, Que.

Quebec City has been called "the oldest continuously inhabited settlement in North America" and "the only walled city on the continent north of Mexico." It is strategically and imposingly situated on the north bank of the St. Lawrence River at the extreme narrowing of the river above Ile d'Orléans. The site was visited by Jacques Cartier in 1535 and settled by Samuel de Champlain in 1608. Champlain called it Québec after *kebek,* the Algonkian word for "strait" or "narrow passage." It became the "cradle" of New France. It reached town status in 1792 and city status in 1833. The present population is 576,075. It is the capital of the Province of Quebec (the 1983 population of which is 6,477,800).

Two distinguished visitors had opposite reactions to Quebec City. Writing in 1883, the American novelist Henry James complained: "Something assures one that Quebec must be a city of gossip; for evidently it is not a city of culture." Writing one year later, the British man-of-letters Matthew Arnold exclaimed: "Quebec is the most interesting thing by much that I have seen on this Continent, and I think I would sooner be a poor priest in Quebec than a rich hog-merchant in Chicago."

There are many reminders in the *rues* of Vieux Québec of the *Ancien Régime.* The visitor is inclined to forget that Quebec City — and not the larger and more dynamic Montreal — is the province's capital. The city's motto, which alludes to the name of Jacques Cartier's ship, is *Don de Dieu Feray Valoir*. The motto translates "God's Gift to Make the Most" — and that is precisely what Quebec City does.

EN BAS
LES ANGLAIS

REGINA, Sask.

It is easy to find Regina — all one has to do is remember that it is located halfway between Winnipeg and Calgary. It was once known as Pile o' Bones, a literal translation of the Cree word *Wascana*. In 1882, Governor General the Marquess of Lorne gave the settlement the name of Regina in honour of Queen Victoria, his mother-in-law. It became a town the following year and a city in 1903. The present population is 164,313.

The site of Regina is flat, as Sir John A.Macdonald noted on his visit in 1886: "If you had a lit-tle more wood, and a lit-tle more water, and here and there a hill, I think the prospect would be improved."

Regina is the capital of the Province of Saskatchewan. This word comes from the Cree *Kisiskatchewani Sipi,* with the meaning of "swift current" or "swift-flowing-river." The city of Swift Current (population 14,264) relects this meaning. The 1983 population of the province is 991,000.

Anagrams of REGINA are EARNING, GAINER, and REGAIN.

ROCKY MOUNTAINS

The earliest reference by name to the Rocky Mountains, the Western Cordillera, appears as *Montagnes de Roche* in 1752. The mountains are renowned for their beauty and look ancient (though to geologists they are relatively young as mountains go). "Behold! The Shining Mountains" is a phrase associated with Anthony Henday, the first known European to see the Rocky Mountains, October 17, 1754. The HBC agent recorded his impressions in a journal (which has not survived) near present-day Innisfail, Alta. The suggestion is that his Indian guides referred to the Rockies as "the Shining Mountains."

The British writer, V.S. Pritchett, in an article published in 1964, was not particularly impressed with the Rockies. He noted: "They are less friendly than the Andes — they are grayer; they lack the urbanity and — I may as well say it — the intelligence of the Alps. This is absurd anthropomorphism, I know, but I am thinking of the poverty of human association in the scene .... "

ST. CATHARINES, Ont.

Two things are peculiar about the spelling of St. Catharines. To the dismay of generations of students, the name of this Ontario city is spelled with two *a's* rather than two *e's*, and there is no apostrophe before the *s*. It was named in 1809 by the merchant Robert Hamilton to honour his wife Catharine Askin Hamilton. Two other names — The Twelve and Shipman's Corners — date back to 1784. St. Catharines became a town in 1850 and a city in 1876. Sometimes it is called "Garden City" and "Capital of the Niagara Fruit Belt." The present population is 134,353.

The city has at least two literary associations. The first is the fact that William Butler Yeats lectured here, for as he explained in a letter written to Lady Gregory on February 13, 1914: "I am at St. Catherine's *(sic)*, the guest of the hotel proprietor, and described last night the theatre of beauty and I think I puzzled the audience." The second item of literary consequence is the use the detective-story writer Howard Engel has made of the downtown area of the city in his Benny Cooperman novels. For the "feel" of the city read *The Suicide Murders* (1980), *The Ransom Game* (1981), and *Murder on Location* (1982).

SAINT JOHN, N.B.

The city was named after the river discovered by Sieur de Monts on the anniversary of St. John the Baptist, June 24, 1604. It was incorporated as a city in 1785, and as such is considered to be the oldest incorporated city in Canada. It is called the "Loyalist City" in recognition of the United Empire Loyalists who settled here and gave the city much of its industrious air. The present population is 114,048.

Donald Sutherland, the movie star, hails from Saint John, and so did actor Walter Pidgeon and movie mogul Louis B. Mayer. (Pidgeon used to joke that the only reason M-G-M gave him a chance was that he came from the boss's hometown.) In 1939, the University of New Brunswick awarded Mayer an honorary doctor of laws. In his convocation address Mayer made a promise: "Each and every year, health permitting, I will return to the university and take part in the Encaenia exercises. At the same time I will take advantage of the opportunity to fish in New Brunswick streams and go back and tell the world what a grand and glorious land this is." Apparently health did not permit, as he never returned to New Brunswick.

Where the first Loyalists waded ashore two centuries ago stands Market Square, the downtown's new shopping and cultural complex.

ST. JOHN'S, Nfld.

The feast of St. John the Baptist is celebrated on June 24, and on this date in the year 1497 it is maintained St. John's was discovered by John Cabot. (The same feast marks the discovery date of the river of its namesake, Saint John,N.B.) In 1583, Sir Humphrey Gilbert came to the site of the future city and claimed the island of Newfoundland on behalf on England. (A few months later, drowning in the Altantic, he was heard to remind his men: "We are as near to heaven by sea as by land!") St. John's was incorporated as a city in 1888 and has a population of 86,576. The historic and salty city makes two claims: it is the oldest inhabited town in North America; it is the most easterly city in North America.

In fact, this was a bustling seaport when Michelangelo was painting the ceiling of the Sistine Chapel. Basques fished the Grand Banks centuries before Columbus made his landfall in the Caribbean, and even earlier Vikings lived and died and gave birth in settlements on the northern reaches of the "Great Island."

St. John's is the capital of Newfoundland which, in 1948, exchanged its status as Britain's oldest colony for the distinction of becoming Canada's youngest province. The provincial population in 1983 is 575,900. "New founde isle" is what John Cabot called this island in 1497, and it became "New found launde" in 1502. About a century later, the poet John Donne wrote about "O my America! my new-found-land" in his poem Elegy XIX (which is about exploring his mistress' body rather than the New World).

ST. LAWRENCE RIVER, Que.

Although not the longest river in Canada — the Mackenzie which flows into the Arctic Ocean has that distinction — the St. Lawrence is the most historic and important. On August 10, 1535, Jacques Cartier named a minor bay for St. Lawrence, whose feast day it was. (He was the martyr who exclaimed to the Romans who were roasting him on a gridiron: "My flesh is well cooked on one side; turn the other, and eat.") Frequently called the Great River of Canada, it played and plays in the national life of the country the role of the Rhine in Germany, the Nile in Egypt, the Mississippi in the United States, the Congo in Africa, and the Yellow River in China. From the westernmost of the Great Lakes to the Atlantic Ocean, it is in length 1900 miles (3058 km).

"An imperial river — the St. Lawrence has always been that," wrote Hugh MacLennan. "The St. Lawrence has made nations. It has been the moulder of the lives of millions of people, perhaps by now of hundreds of millions ... " And to Walt Whitman, one of the wonders of Canada was "the magnificent St. Lawrence itself .... "

Rabelais, in Book IV of *Gargantua and Pantagruel* (1552), has the giant Gargantua venture up the St. Lawrence until he comes to the island which he calls the country of "frozen words." It is so cold here — spiritually and climatically — that the very words freeze in the air, and must be thawed out to be heard.

SAINT-LOUIS-DU-HA! HA!, Que.

An actual community on the south shore of the St. Lawrence, inland from Rivière-du-Loup by 37 miles (60 km), bears this unusual name. It was named in honour of St. Louis and in memory of Louis Marquis, the first settler. It has been suggested that Saint-Louis-du-Ha! Ha! is the only place name in the world with an official designation that includes two exclamations.

On the north shore, the Saguenay River has a tributary, Ha! Ha! River, with a bay, Ha! Ha! Bay. Walt Whitman visited Ha! Ha! Bay in August 1880 and wrote in his diary: "Up the black Saguenay River, a hundred or so miles — a dash of the grimmest, wildest, savagest scenery on the planet, I guess; a strong, deep (always hundreds of feet, sometimes thousands), dark-water'd river, very dark, with high rocky hills, green and gray edged banks in all directions — no flowers, no fruits ...."

SASKATOON, Sask.

Saskatoon, after Regina, is the largest city in Saskatchewan. It is located on the South Saskatchewan River and takes its name from the Cree word *Mis-sask-quah-too-min* for an edible red berry that grows in the area. The site was established by the Temperance Colonization Society. It was settled in 1883, became a village in 1901, a town in 1903, and a city in 1906. Population today is 154,210

John G. Diefenbaker enjoyed telling the story of the two Englishwomen who were travelling by train across the country. "Where are we now?" asked the first. "I don't know," replied the second, "but when we come to the next station, I will get off and ask." When the train stopped, the woman got off and asked the first person she met where they were. "Saskatoon, Saskatchewan," was the reply. She boarded the train. "Well," asked the first woman, "where are we?" "I don't know," replied the second, "all they speak here is Indian."

Sir Harry Lauder, the celebrated Scots singer and entertainer, composed one of his most popular songs in Saskatoon during a blizzard. This is "Granny's Laddie," about a young soldier whose "hair was fair and his eyes were blue."

STRATFORD, Ont.

"How nice" was Sir Laurence Olivier's measured response when Tom Patterson suggested that he help found a Shakespearian festival in this small Ontario city. The following year, on July 13, 1952, the Stratford Festival opened, with Alec Guinness (and not Sir Laurence) playing Richard the Third.

Stratford was known as Little Thames until 1831 when it acquired its present name. Earlier someone had named the picturesque river the Avon. Both names echo William Shakespeare's birthplace of Stratford-on-Avon. It became a village in 1854, a town in 1859, and a city in 1885. The present population is 25,657. Until the founding of the Stratford Festival, the city was known principally as the home town of hockey player Howie Morenz (the "Stratford Streak") and the scene of the Stratford Strike of 1933, during which woodworkers picketed and the authorities introduced troops, machine guns, and even tanks. These days the only weapons of any sort seen in the city are on stage — bows and arrows, swords and shields, etc.

SWASTIKA, Ont.

Swastika was the name of a small mining community in northern Ontario long before Adolf Hitler chose the swastika, or twisted cross of Aryan mythology, as the Nazi emblem. Who named the community, or why, is not known, but the first record of the name is 1906. With the discovery of gold five years later, nearby Kirkland Lake expanded. Swastika is now part of Kirkland Lake, and the combined population is 12,219.

In the early years of World War II, Mitch Hepburn, Premier of Ontario, decided the name Swastika was unpatriotic, so he lobbied to change the name of the post office to Winston, to honour wartime leader Winston Churchill. But the people thought otherwise, and at a public meeting on September 13, 1940, resisted the change. Speakers pointed out that their use of the name predated Hitler's and would certainly postdate it as well. They maintained that their patriotism was unimpaired.

The inhabitants of Swastika, right on both counts, won the day. Yet there is the possibility of a real though tenuous connection between the place and the Nazi Party. It is not at all clear how Hitler learned of the twisted cross. One suggestion is that he heard of it from his "Nordic goddess," Unity Mitford, who certainly knew of it from her father, Lord Redesdale the eccentric British peer who for some time lived in a log cabin just outside Swastika. If so, it is an irony of history that the Ontario community contributed the twisted cross to the arsenal of Nazi symbology.

SYDNEY, N.S.

Located on the northeastern coast of Cape Breton Island, of which it is the chief city, Sydney was named after Thomas Townsend, first Viscount Sydney, in 1785. A town in 1885, a city in 1904, it has a population today of 87,489. Two other communities are North Sydney and Sydney Mines.

Sydney was once the capital of the old province of Cape Breton. Today the basis of the economy is coal, steel, and tourism. Al Boliska, the comedy writer, put the world into perspective when he quipped, "Contrary to popular opinion, if you went to Sydney,

Nova Scotia, and dug a hole straight through the earth, you would not end up in China. Due to the rotation of the earth, on its axis, you would come out in Pefferlaw, Ontario."

THUNDER BAY, Ont.

Thunder Bay, at the head of Lake Superior, recalls *Animikie wekwed,* the Algonkian thunderbird, so the name should really be Thunder Bird Bay. The present name was chosen from that of the district in 1970 with the amalgamation of Fort William (named after NWC president William McGillivray) and Port Arthur (after Prince Arthur, Duke of Connaught). The present city has a population of 121,379.

The thunderbird may not be much in evidence, but Nanabozho is. The so-called Sleeping Giant is visible from the city; offshore is a promontory 1,000 feet high and 7 miles long with the outline of a reclining giant. In imagination the figure, the legendary Nanabozho, threatens to rise, as native legends predict he will, to sweep injustice from the world.

In 1873, Susanna Moodie received a letter from her daughter which read: "If I were an artist I would choose Thunder Bay in a storm as the grandest representation of the end of the world. I could not help fancying when I looked over the side of the vessel that I could see old Charon launch his boat from the foot of Thunder Cape. Thunder Bay would be a magnificent Styx."

In 1908, Rudyard Kipling visited Fort William and Port Arthur and explained: "Two towns stand on the shores of the lake less than a mile apart. What Lloyds is to shipping, or the College of Surgeons to medicine, that they are to the Wheat. Its honour and integrity are in their hands; and they hate each other with the pure, poisonous, passionate hatred which makes towns grow."

TORONTO, Ont.

This Indian word has been variously translated. "Place of meeting" is the official meaning in the language of the Hurons, though to the Wyandots it could signify "place of plenty." Both interpretations make sense. Since 1656, when it first appeared on an European map, the place has been known as: Tarantou, Teioiagon, Fort Rouille, York, Little York, Muddy York, Muddy Little York, Toronto, Toronto the Good, City of Churches, Babylon-on-the-Humber, Hogtown, Sin City, The City that Works, and now People City.

Toronto became a city with its present name in 1834, so the year 1984 marked its sesquicentennial or 150th anniversary. Since the mid-1960s, it has been Canada's largest city, with a 1983 population of 2,998,947. It serves as the capital of the Province of Ontario — Ontario, by the way, means "sparkling water" — and as the communications centre of Canada. Ontario's population was, in 1983, 8,753,600.

Not everyone approved of the place. George Wookcock, the Vancouver author, "rather dislikes" it. Aleister Crowley, the British occultist, claimed "it is a calculated crime both against the aspirations of the soul and the affection of the heart." To Rupert Brooke "the only depressing thing is that it will always be what it is, only larger." Charles Dickens found it "full of life and motion, bustle, business, and improvement." Walt Whitman had "memories of a very lively and agreeable visit," whereas Wyndham Lewis, who lived here, wrote that "Toronto is probably not a good place to be an intellectual in." Yet Northrop Frye explained, "Toronto is an excellent town to mind one's business in." What Torontonians hold dear are the malapropisms of its one-time mayor Allan Lamport, who has been called "Metro's Goldwyn Mayor" for such observations as "No one should ever visit Toronto for the first time" and "Toronto is the city of the future — and always will be."

TROIS-RIVIÈRES, Que.

Question: Which river branches into three where it meets the St. Lawrence?

Answer: La Rivière Saint-Maurice.

TORONTO

TORONTO

TORONTO

TORONTO

TORONTO

The delta-like islands formed by the Saint-Maurice River were visited by Jacques Cartier in 1535. The area was settled in 1643 and incorporated as a city in 1857. Trois-Rivières — which Anglophones once resolutely called Three Rivers — is an important port for pulp and paper. The present population is 111,453.

Maurice Duplessis, born at Trois-Rivières, favoured the place of his birth. (It is worthy of note perhaps, that the long-time Premier of Quebec was born on April 20, 1890, the birthday of Nazi dictator Adolf Hitler.) Duplessis was given to puns, if not guns. In 1956, he punned on the St. Maurice River and Prime Minister Louis St. Laurent. "You all know that the St. Maurice hurls itself into the St. Lawrence, but have you ever heard of the St. Laurent rising up from its bed to inundate the St. Maurice? As long as the St. Laurent and the St. Maurice flow their respective courses, all will be well."

TUKTOYAKTUK, N.W.T.

Tuktoyaktuk — or Tuk for short — is a weather station, DEW line installation, RCMP post, post office, mission centre, and trading post on the Beaufort Sea east of the mouth of the Mackenzie River. Despite so much activity, Tuk is a hamlet with a population of only 772. Before 1950, it was known as Fort Brabant. The Inuktitut name means "reindeer that looks like caribou."

VANCOUVER, B.C.

"Vancouver it shall be," declared Sir William Van Horne, and in 1886 it acquired its present name and city status. The railroad builder was honouring Captain George Vancouver who had explored and mapped the Pacific Coast of North America in 1792-93.

Vancouver's location on Burrard Inlet at the mouth of the Fraser River and its natural beauty have helped it grow to become the third-largest of Canada's cities and, in the opinion of many, its most beautiful. The population is 1,268,183. Rudyard Kipling bought land here and apparently George Bernard Shaw gave more than passing thought to settling in Vancouver. During the Battle of

Britain, he wrote to a resident: "So far we have not budged a step, and shall not unless Hitler pushes us out by the scruffs of our necks. In that case we shall certainly come to Canada, as we have a joint annuity there to die on. And Vancouver is the pick of Canada .... "

There is no definition of a Vancouverite, but Allan Fotheringham (the columnist known as "the Wicked Wit of the West") maintains: "In Vancouver, an 'outsider' is anyone living six miles or more from the ocean."

Does anyone know how the following limerick ends? "There was an old maid of Vancouver/Who was raped by J. Edgar Hoover .... "

VICTORIA, B.C.

Fort Albert, Fort Camosun, and Fort Victoria are early names of Victoria, which was chosen in 1843 to honour the young Queen of England. (Virtually every province has a village, town, or city honouring the Dowager Empress.) Victoria, which is located on the southeastern extremity of Vancouver Island overlooking the Strait of Juan de Fuca, became a city in 1862. The population is 233,481.

Well and truly named, Victoria has many Victorian aspects: the floral displays of Butchart Gardens, mock-Tudor architecture, high tea (Murchie's) and chocolate (Rogers) at the Empress Hotel, and a mild climate so appreciated by the English folk and so delightfully drawn by cartoonist Len Norris.

Rudyard Kipling wrote in 1908: "Canada possesses two pillars of Strength and Beauty in Quebec and Victoria. The former ranks by herself among those Mother-cities of whom none can say 'This reminds me.' To realize Victoria you must take all that the eye admires most in Bournemouth, Torquay, the Isle of Wight, the Happy Valley of Hong Kong, the Doon, Sorrento, and Camps Bay; add reminiscences of the Thousand Islands, and arrange the whole round the Bay of Naples, with some Himalayas for the background."

Victoria is the capital of the Province of British Columbia which had a 1983 population of 2,800,500. Simon Fraser Tolmie, premier from 1928 to 1933, maintained: "British Columbia is Canada's westernmost province and geographic centre of the British Empire." Humourist Eric Nicol described his province as "the first one on the left."

Outpost
XLVIII

WAWA, Ont.

The Ojibwa word for "goose" or "wild goose" is *wawa*, and just outside the community of Wawa on the Trans-Canada Highway north of Lake Superior stands a giant, thirty-foot steel sculpture of a goose. It is an inspiring sight, but had the executives of the Algoma Steel Corporation had their way, instead of a giant goose there would have been standing there a thirty-foot statue of Sir James Dunn, the company's principal shareholder. The company lobbied from 1948 to 1953 to have the name of the community changed from Wawa to Jamestown, but a plebiscite defeated the move — though it was not until 1960 that Wawa's name was confirmed once and for all.

WHITEHORSE, Y.T.

Whitehorse was named for the nearby Whitehorse Rapids which are said to resemble in whiteness the mane of a white horse. The rapids are part of the Yukon River which has been so important in the development of the Yukon Territory.

The name goes back to the Klondike Gold Rush, and there are many reminders here of the Trail of '98, including Sam McGee's Cabin, familiar to readers of Robert Service's mighty poem "The Cremation of Sam McGee." The present population is 14,814.

Since 1953 the city has been the capital of the Yukon Territory, the 1983 population of which is 23,200. The word Yukon has some interesting derivations. It is generally considered to mean "great river," from the Alaskan Indian word *Yu-kun-ah.* But it may also mean, according to the anthropologist John J. Honigman, "northern lights" *(yokaan)* or "wicked ones" *(yuki)* from the language of the Athapascan Indians.

WINDSOR, Ont.

Windsor is Canada's most southern city, on the same approximate latitude as Sofia and Tashkent. Indeed, by its location on the south bank of the Detroit River, it is located *south* of the city of Detroit. Windsor is a border city *par excellence,* boasting from the foot of Ouellette Avenue an unparalleled view of the Detroit skyline (with its Renaissance Centre).

Windsor was named after the Royal seat in England in 1834, becoming a village in 1854, a town in 1858, a city in 1892. The present population is 246,110. Official rhetoric has it that Windsor is "The City of the Roses" (and bar-room bombast counters with "the armpit of Canada").

One of its noted citizens, Paul Martin, whenever he delivered an address in a distant part of the world, would ask, "Is there anybody here from Windsor?"

WINNIPEG, Man.

The meaning of the Cree word that is the basis of the name Winnipeg is *Win-nipi* for Lake Winnipeg which has the unfortunate meaning of "dirty water" or "murky water." In the same way Lake Winnipegosis comes from the Cree for "little muddy water." Located at the junction of the Assiniboine and Red rivers, it goes back to the Red River Settlement of 1811-12. It was incorporated as a city in 1873 and amalgamation and expansion occurred in 1960 and 1971. The current population is 584,842.

The Peg, as it is sometimes called, is the capital of the Province of Manitoba. The word Manitoba also comes from the Cree — *manito-wapow* — for "the strait of the spirit," a reference to the Narrows of Lake Manitoba. (The more familiar form of the Indian word is *Manitou*, for the spirit or mystery.) The provincial population in 1983 was 1,042,500.

The story is told of the rookie correspondent covering the Winnipeg Flood of May 1950 who cabled his London editor: GOD LOOKED DOWN FROM THE PEMBINA HILLS NEAR WINNIPEG TODAY ON AN AWESOME SCENE OF DESTRUCTION .... The editor wired back: FORGET FLOOD. INTERVIEW GOD.

In 1960, in *Scotchman's Return*, Hugh MacLennan bemoaned the lack of interest shown by Canadians in their own cities. He epitomized this in the title of one of his essays: "Boy Meets Girl in Winnipeg and Who Cares?"

The windiest intersection in all of Canada is said to be Portage and Main in downtown Winnipeg. Here, the story goes, the prevailing winds over the last forty years have shifted the entire intersection six inches to the west.

YELLOWKNIFE, N.W.T.

Situated on the north shore of Great Slave Lake, Yellowknife is only 320 miles (512 km) south of the Arctic Circle. One would assume its name stems from the gold discovery in 1934, from which settlement dates, but this is not so, for it comes from the colour of the copper worked by the Copper and Athapaskan Indians. Yellowknife was incorporated as a city in 1970 and has a population of 9,483.

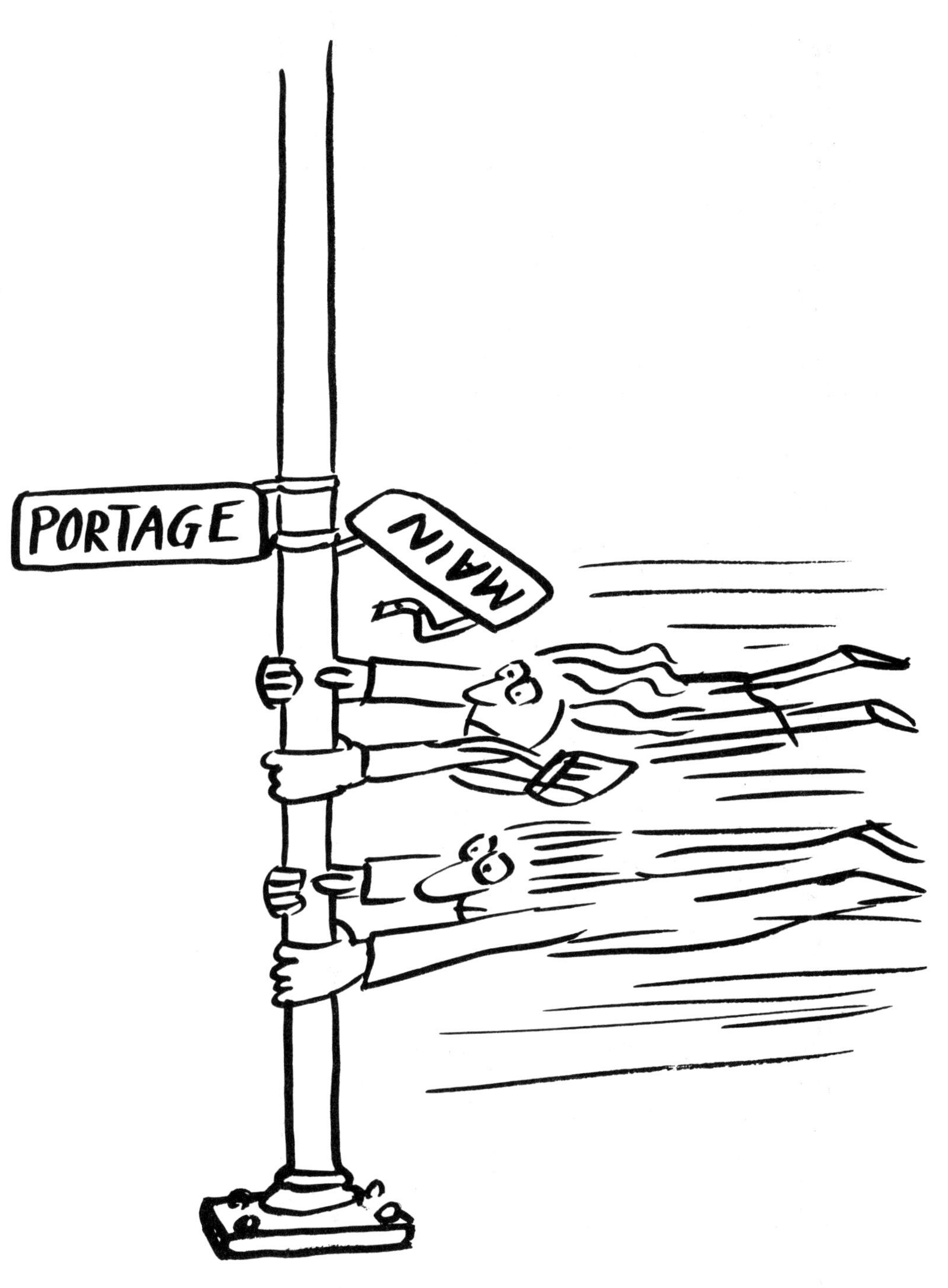
PORTAGE
MAIN

Yellowknife is the capital and chief city of the Northwest Territories. The Territories consist of three Districts: Franklin (named after the Arctic explorer), Keewatin (after the Cree for "north wind"), and Mackenzie (Sir Alexander Mackenzie the explorer). All three Districts are north and west of Lake Superior — hence the name. Residents voted favourably in a plebiscite in 1982 to divide the N.W.T. into two parts, Nunavut and Denendeh. The population in 1983 was 47,400.

As Farley Mowat wrote in *Tundra* (1973): "I have my own vision of the high North. I envision it being transformed — restored — into a symbol of sanity in a world where madness is becoming the accepted mode of action."

YOHO NATIONAL PARK, B.C.

Yoho National Park, a wilderness area of 507 square miles (1,313 km^2), is in British Columbia. It is adjacent to Alberta and Banff National Park. The word Yoho identifies a station, a glacier, a lake, a mountain, a pass, a river, and a valley, in addition to a park. The pleasant sound brings to mind a call for attention, a Swiss yodel, and the nautical cry "Yo-heave-ho!" It is said to be the Cree word for "How wonderful."

How wonderful! What an appropriate way to sound the note to end this canter across the country.

Mount YOHO
YOHO
LAKE YOHO
YOHO Valley
YOHO ke Field

ATLAS
Canada

Colombo's
101 CANADIAN PLACES